After forty years of psychiatric practice, I have learned that people thrive better in community. Marriage is an environment that can foster intimate community or painful isolation. This book is a guided tour toward building an enduring marital community through the many seasons of life.

*— Michael R. Lyles, MD, Diplomate of the American Board of Psychiatry and Neurology, Speaker and Author*

I have been privileged to know about Gene Schrader's biblically-based counseling ministry for many years, and his book *Intimacy Lost and Found* well encapsulates the essence of his life-giving encounters in the lives of others. This book is based on Gene's rich counseling experience and is illustrated with stories about forgiveness, boundaries, and reconciliation. It clearly develops the significance of grasping a biblical self-image as part of God's design for loving and intimate relationships.

*— Dr. Kenneth Boa, President of Reflections Ministries, Author of more than 50 books, including* **Conformed to His Image** *and* **Serious Business of Heaven**

Identity is being stolen from us today in every way. Our identity is uniquely crafted by God for each of us. These pages articulate the freedom found in your true identity from your creator. I watched my daughter get set free by Gene's vulnerability and carefully crafted stories filled with practically applied wisdom.

One cannot fully lead others until they know the source of their true Identity. The content of this book will help you reach your full potential in Christ and be freed from any lies that have hindered your joy.

Thank you, Gene Schrader, for being a pioneer and a forerunner in rescuing people from brokenness into leadership!

*— Catherine Webb Williams, former executive leader for Gillette, GE, and Adecco, currently the CEO of a privately held global consulting firm*

The raw transparency and venerability from the author sets the tone for readers to easily access deep biblical truths in the midst of deep pain. Our counseling journey with Gene was nearly 45 years ago as we struggled in our marriage. Jan and I rejoice as we just happily celebrated our 50th wedding anniversary with Gene and Eldeen. The truths of intimacy outlined in this book are a must read.

*— Ed and Jan Butler, Elder and Lay Counselors*

Intimacy Lost *and* Found

Restoring God's Design for
Closeness in a Disconnected Marriage

# *Intimacy*
## Lost *and* Found

## Gene Schrader, LMFT

BookJourney

Library of Congress Control Number: 2025945779

ISBN (hardcover): 978-1-968737-16-0

ISBN (paperback): 978-1-968737-02-3

ISBN (ebook): 978-1-968737-03-0

Cover design by Bridget Walton

Interior typesetting and design by Young Design

Book Journey

Published by Book Journey Publishing

Castle Rock, Colorado, USA

Bookjourney.com

# Contents

# Dedication

*To my wife, Eldeen, for her faithfulness
and to our loving, supportive children,
grandchildren, and great grandchild*

# Disclaimer

With the exception of the author's immediate family members and quotes from published authors, all names and identifying details of people, locations, institutions, and identifying characteristics have been changed or fictionalized, and certain individuals and conversations are composites, to protect the privacy of individuals involved. The dialogue and events have been recreated, and in some cases have been compressed to convey the substance of what was said or what occurred. Any resemblance to real persons, living or dead, or to actual places or organizations or conversations is purely coincidental. This book is for informational purposes only and does not constitute legal, financial, psychological, marital, and/or medical advice.

# Foreword

*by Deanna Schrader Cunningham*

M ANY YEARS ago I came across Proverbs 17:6, and the second part of the verse captured my attention. "Children's children are a crown to the aged, and parents are the pride of their children." Proverbs are defined as short sentences drawn from long experience, a truth couched in a form that is easy to remember. For me this Proverb has significant meaning. It speaks to my experience, as I am the second-born daughter of Gene and Eldeen Schrader. I am blessed and proud to call them my parents, but also my dearest friends.

The wisdom and truth-filled principles that you will read in this book are intermingled with stories of many people, including the story of my parents' relationship. My father states that "truth is never optional; timing and method are." I cannot remember when my parents shared their background, but I know it was not hidden. Shining a light into darkness, not hiding the past, allowed the light to shine brighter.

When I was eight years old, my father went back to school to get his master's degree in counseling. Every evening as I went to bed, he studied in his office right next to my room.

To some children, this memory might have meant nothing, but to me it burned a special place in my memory. I think that's because it meant he was near (I loved the intimate moments of communication before he went into the office), but also that he was a hard worker committed to doing what God asked of him—even if it meant working long hours to provide for his family and late nights of study as he pursued a new career in obedience to God.

My father has now been a Marriage and Family Therapist for more than forty-five years. This is often unheard of in the field of therapy. When I talk with other counselors and tell them how many years he has counseled more than forty people a week, they are astounded and proclaim their admiration. Remarkably, today in his eighties, he still sees clients regularly. He often says that as long as he is able and God brings people, he will continue to do what he has been called to do. His tenacity, work ethic, and love of God and others have been a hallmark of his life and career.

Throughout my life, whenever someone has told me they know my father, or someone has come up to him in public when I am with him, I have refrained from asking the nature of their relationship. So often they will proceed to tell me how he counseled them or someone they know. Many of his clients have later become his friends. His care and unconditional love are authentic. Recently, I attended a gathering in another area of the city and reconnected with a woman who has been a longtime friend of my parents. I was uncertain of the details of their friendship, just that I had known her since I was young. This woman explained that many years ago my father helped save her marriage. She went on to share that on the anniversary of their marriage, every year for the past twenty years, she has sent my father a thank you note. I cannot tell you how many times I have had similar things happen to me over the years.

I want you to know that I personally have been privileged to watch both my parents live out the truths they share in this book. They are human and real, not perfect. Yet, their steadfast, unconditional love and pursuit of God's heart and truth have had a profound impact on their children and their children's children. I get a little emotional as I remember the times they have intentionally, prayerfully loved me and our family. I have even followed in my dad's footsteps by pursuing a master's degree in counseling as well.

Based on their backgrounds, this could easily have been a different outcome for my parents. I found a quote regarding the proverb I mentioned which states that "Behind this apparently innocuous proverb is a profound assertion of the psychological interdependence of the generations. Elders derive a sense of pride from their descendants, and children get their self-worth from parents. On the other hand, one generation can cause shame and a sense of worthlessness in another."[1]

When I share my story, I often start with theirs. Their decisions and choices changed the trajectory of our lives. We still had and have to make our own decisions, but they opened the doors for us to understand intimacy with our Heavenly Father, as well as what intimacy in marriage, family, and friendships involves.

While some of the stories shared are dramatic or intense, the principles remain true in any relationship. As my husband and I are coming up on thirty-six years of marriage, we, too, have to be reminded of these truths. Marriage is wonderful and hard. Because God desires to bring two people into the intimacy of marriage so He may be glorified, Satan intensely works to destroy marriage. The battle does not go away but requires a continual surrender to God and His truth.

I encourage you to read this book if you are in crisis in your marriage. But even if you are not in crisis and desire to understand intimacy and want to equip yourself to walk in true intimacy in your life, you will discover life-proven, time-tested truths within these pages.

# Note from Author

For those walking tender paths of healing—through wounds seen and unseen, prayers whispered in the quiet, and hope that feels fragile yet alive—this book is for you.

As you read, know that my prayers surround you, that your heart may find rest, your spirit be gently restored, and that you may be drawn into a deeper, abiding intimacy with Jesus.

# Part One

## In the Beginning the Connection Was Perfect

*Beautiful truth about intimacy—*
*What it is and why God designed it*

CHAPTER 1

# Uniquely Common

OVER THE past forty-some years in the counseling room, I have seen about every kind of personality, background, and experience in life you can imagine, and one thing is common in us all—a desire to be loved. Each of us longs for someone who will always be there for us, someone who will stay with us when everyone else leaves us flat. We want someone we are free to be ourselves with, someone who knows everything about us and still loves us, someone we can connect with on a deep, soul level. What we want is intimacy.

Tragically, our present culture defines intimacy as solely sexual. The common belief rampant among our society is that our desire for intimacy can be satisfied through a physical sexual encounter. However, the truth is quite the opposite. Intimate sex is the *result* of authentic intimacy—not a means to it. But our culture perpetuates its lie, and sex is reduced to an animalistic interchange, immorality rather than intimacy. Orgasm is held to be the height of intimacy, leaving countless individuals feeling hurt and disconnected. Husbands and wives who rely on physical intimacy alone for connection will find themselves headed toward relationship failure, whether the marriage drags on disconnected or ends in dismay.

Many couples realize there is more to being close than physical affection yet still struggle to achieve true intimacy. Too often, spouses live lonely lives within a marriage, sometimes burdened by the additional devastation of unfaithfulness and broken dreams of what could have been.

So we have to ask the questions: With all of the relationship failures, hurts, and betrayals, is intimacy in marriage something we can actually hope to find? Or is it just a fantasy that nobody ever gets to live? Is authentic intimacy forever lost?

In my own marriage, as well as countless others I've had the privilege of working with in therapy, I can assure you intimacy is available to us all. In the pages ahead, I will show you the beautiful truth about intimacy, what it is and why God designed it, what causes us to lose or not experience intimacy, and how to restore true intimacy within our marriages.

I have counseled numerous couples who were in marriages "beyond hope." We searched for answers and connected with new challenges, and we pressed on, week after week. Thankfully, many of the husbands and wives I have worked with didn't divorce and are now experiencing a level of intimacy they never thought possible. God's desire is to break through the deception and pain, through the fear of intimacy in the marriage, and to restore a divine closeness that meets the intimacy needs of both husband and wife.

Scripture is clear about God's design for man and woman to live together in holy, intimate matrimony, not to divorce. However, there are times when divorce is unavoidable. This is a devastating loss, to be sure, but a marriage without intimacy is in itself a tremendous loss.

I recognize we live in a fallen world where we have learned to fear intimacy. This paradox exists within each of us: the longing to connect at a deep human level and a strong fear of being hurt. No one escapes being hurt when attempting to be intimate. That's because we are attempting to connect with imperfect people, just like us. By nature, our inner self hides, blames others, and runs from self-exposure. And yet, we were created to experience intimacy.

> This paradox exists within each of us: the longing to connect at a deep human level and a strong fear of being hurt.

So is there hope as we attempt to connect? Can we really experience true intimacy? Absolutely, yes! That is why I am writing this book. To give you hope and to show you the way to experiencing authentic intimacy in your marriage. Together we will explore the experiences that have threatened your ability to be intimate. We will discover how to break the chains of pain and fear, and we will learn how, through

God's power, to bring restoration into your marriage relationship. The road to true intimacy may look a little scary, but I promise you—it leads to where you have always longed to go.

## Dreams of Intimacy

We all want to be loved by that one special someone, and we long to love that person with our whole heart in return. Each of us desires intimacy. We dream of whispered secrets, shared hopes, fulfilled desires, a relationship where we can be transparent, vulnerable, truly ourselves, knowing deep in our hearts we are safe with our loved one. Those dreams begin at childhood, and we nurture them until the day we finally meet that one person who is destined to be our spouse, the answer to our loneliness, the fulfiller of our intimate wishes.

What we don't anticipate is the inevitable hurt and disappointment that comes with being in an intimate relationship with another imperfect human being. This is common to us all. We all experience being hurt by someone we love, someone we believed had our highest and best purposes in mind, someone we trusted to be there for us. Then, by either commission or omission (something they did or did not do, intentional or not), they let us down. This could range from being deserted in time of need to outright betrayal. Feelings get hurt, promises are broken, expectations unmet. No married couple avoids the pain of being hurt by one another.

Some husbands and wives are fortunate. These wise couples quickly recognize their hurtful actions or words and the damage they cause, then enter into forgiveness, learning how to avoid similar hazards going forward. For others, however, unavoidable pain and disconnect make intimacy nearly impossible. If this is you today, I pray you continue reading and that you will find hope as I (Gene) share God's truth for intimacy, alongside stories of other couples and individuals who have been where you are.

The following story reflects countless others I've heard in my counseling office over the years. Read on as a devastated wife pours out her heart, confessing her deep hurt.

*In the beginning, I thought I had married a king. When we were in high school, my husband-to-be was crowned homecoming king of our senior class. He chose me, a princess in the court, as his date that evening. That was our first date. Romantic, isn't it? I sure thought so.*

*After dating for three years, we got married. It didn't take long for me to think I might have made a big mistake. On our honeymoon, he told me he had been seeing another woman during our engagement. I was furious. Now he tells me!*

*Our first year of marriage was very difficult for me. My husband still had a year of college to complete, so we set up house off campus. While I knew only a few people on a casual basis, my husband was quite established socially as the president of his fraternity. Drinking played a big part in this social structure. I began to wonder if I had married an alcoholic.*

*I was lonely. I was miserable. And three months after we*

*were married, I was pregnant. This was not joyous news to me at the time. Financially, we were not ready for a baby. And on top of it, I felt like my husband was not the man I had married. Before we got married, he pursued me and showed interest in me. Now he was spending most of his time drinking with his buddies. He felt distant and disconnected from me.*

*We had our first daughter, and then two years later daughter number two arrived. By this time, things were a bit better. My husband was doing well in business. We had a nice home, a nice car, and could take nice vacations. Our life structure was stable, even if it lacked the intimacy I longed for.*

"Things were a bit better," this hurting woman said. What does that mean, exactly? Not as much conflict, perhaps? Or maybe this young wife and mother had resigned to the sad prospect she would never experience true intimacy with her husband, yet things were "good enough" to stay put. And that's where her marriage sat, lacking the closeness, the intimacy, she craved—the intimacy she needed.

How many spouses find themselves in this same place? I've heard so many comments from a wounded husband or distressed wife that reveal a heart that is discontent, lonely in marriage, disconnected from the partner who promised to love and cherish till death do us part.

"It's not that bad."

"At least he doesn't hit me."

"It could be worse, I suppose."

"Our sex is good, so I guess that counts for something."

That's not intimacy, and that's not what God wants for you in your marriage.

## Sex is Intimate, Not Intimacy

Let's begin by taking a look at what intimacy is and what it isn't. When a married couple lives in intimacy, they operate in openness, transparency, the freedom to be themselves. They open their hearts freely to one another because they trust each other. Their hearts know they are safe, so there is no need to put up a wall to protect themselves from their marriage partner. And since there is nothing to hide, these intimate couples can be completely transparent with one another. That is pure openness. They confess the vulnerable and honest parts of themselves within the safety of an authentically intimate relationship, knowing they are loved no matter what.

Transparency provides an open window to the heart, with nothing held back or covered up. When each spouse knows in their heart they are loved, because their openness and transparency have been met with complete acceptance, they are free to be themselves with no fear of rejection, judgment, or disapproval. That is the beauty of authentic intimacy. True intimacy is a safe closeness that connects to the soul and extends way beyond a physical attachment.

> *Transparency provides an open window to the heart, with nothing held back or covered up.*

It is important to note that our sexuality is 3-D. By that, I mean we are three-dimensional beings—mental, emotional, and physical. When we engage in physical sex (in or outside of marriage), our whole soul is involved—the mental and emotional along with the physical. But just because our soul is involved, that doesn't mean it is automatically connecting with the other person. Yes, the body might connect, but all the while the soul can remain distant. Only when the soul, your true inner self, feels fully known and truly, safely loved by the other person can it connect in intimacy.

*True intimacy is a safe closeness that connects to the soul and extends way beyond a physical attachment.*

Sex by itself will not bring us to a connection at a deeper level, regardless of what our society tells us. To have intimacy in sex requires intimacy in the relationship—a knowing, an understanding, a commitment of love and faithfulness. That kind of intimacy simply cannot happen through a physical act alone. Yes, sex is intimate on a physical level as the body responds to sexual stimulation, but if the soul isn't connected, the sexual act is not initiating intimacy. Even some rape victims are known to have orgasms against their will when an intimate act is forced upon them. The body responds even while the soul is being crushed. That is one of the worst violations of an intimate act, and it is not intimacy by any means. God has made us as sexual beings, but sexual intimacy as God designed it only occurs within the safety of a loving, committed marriage. Only in the context of marriage can a man and woman truly become one, in all three dimensions. This beautiful intimacy is truly a miracle and a mystery in this imperfect world.

When we try to meet our sexual needs outside of God's way, true intimacy cannot be shared. I have asked every woman (generally speaking, men tend to not be as open with me or as in touch with their inner selves) I have counseled who had a pre- or extra-marital sexual relationship this question: "When you were involved in this sexual encounter, did you totally give yourself to the other person?" The answer is always "no." They were not free to truly give themselves. That's because they were not operating in the safe place of intimacy that God designed for man and wife.

And listen carefully here: Just because a couple is married doesn't mean their sex is truly intimate. If a married couple isn't connecting in authentic intimacy at the soul level in their relationship, they are not connecting in authentic intimacy in sex. The soul knows when it isn't connecting. That's a big disconnect, and that disconnection is painful.

True intimacy in the bedroom comes when a couple shares a bond of true intimacy in their relationship, when they connect vulnerably, openly, at the heart level, with a lifetime commitment of love. Beautiful, authentic sexual intimacy is the result of a beautiful, authentic relational intimacy. That's quite a different picture than the one blasted before us on the movie screen portraying instant intimacy the instant a couple jumps in bed together. Instant intimacy through sex is a dangerous lie, and sadly our culture has bought into it.

Why does our media perpetuate this lie? Because it resonates with the need of every adult.

We are all unique human beings with varying personalities and dreams, but one thing we all have in common is the need to be loved. Each of us longs for an intimate partner to walk through life with, someone who knows us deeply and loves us unconditionally, someone we can love just as wholeheartedly in return. A mutual, healthy, sincere, and solid commitment. Sounds ideal, doesn't it? That kind of marriage relationship falls right in line with God's plan. And that is the kind of intimacy in marriage I will help you work toward in this book.

Here is the reality we face: Since we are all unique, we approach life with our unique set of thoughts and preferences. For example, a young bride may have unspoken expectations that her groom will continue to initiate romantic date nights like he did while they were dating. He, on the other hand, is relieved to be able to cuddle up at home together, no longer having to return his beloved to her own home at the end of the evening. Why go out? If not communicated, these expectations cause conflict for the young couple. Like this example, many conflicts can be resolved or even avoided in the first place through effective communication.

But what about when deeper, more vulnerable expectations are unmet? What happens when faithfulness is replaced with betrayal? What do you do when your marriage isn't securely rooted in mutual respect or trust? When expectations for authentic intimacy fall short, the marriage suffers a deadly blow.

That's what happened to our young wife from the beginning of this chapter.

*Then my "nice" dream for my marriage was shattered. During one of his business trips, my husband was unfaithful. He had betrayed me....*

I have heard this type of story so many times in the counseling room. Oh, the details vary. But the pain and heartache from betrayal is the same. In this particular case, however, for me the pain is double-edged. You see, the story comes from my wife, Eldeen. I had betrayed her.

## Doomed Double Life

At the time, I had no earthly or human understanding of why I was unfaithful to Eldeen. It was plain, unadulterated lust. Lust is instant gratification—wanting something God hasn't given. For some reason I didn't understand at the time, I also had an intense drive to achieve, conquer, win. If you had asked me back then to describe intimacy, I doubt I would have had an answer. Probably I would have said sex. Relational intimacy with my wife wasn't on my radar; winning was everything.

Vince Lombardi once said, "The object is to win—to beat the other guy."[2] That thought burned in my brain. *If only one is going to win, that one is going to be me!* In college, I achieved All-American honors in football and was inducted into the

Carthage Athletic Hall of Fame. In business, I became the number one salesman nationwide within my company. My total focus during this time was providing financially for my family. I was driven to succeed. That didn't leave much room for investing in authentic intimacy with my wife.

I was indeed living a double life. I had been secretly seeing another woman during our engagement. I wouldn't say we were dating; it was more just hanging out together. She pursued me and I liked the pursuit, being tempted with lust, nothing more. I never considered breaking up with Eldeen to date this other woman. But then the other woman showed up to our wedding in a bold dress, which made a statement in 1963. Already drunk, my fraternity brothers pointed and laughed at my ex-girlfriend as my new bride walked down the aisle. To not be distracted by my unruly buddies, I looked up at the ceiling instead of at my beautiful wife-to-be.

That evening, Eldeen asked me why I didn't look at her when she walked down the aisle. I felt so guilty that I confessed the truth of the ill-timed fling. It made me feel so much better not to have to hide my secrecy anymore, but it wasn't true repentance. At the time, I was very immature. I had no concept of sin or of a relationship with God. That didn't come until years later when I finally surrendered my life to the Lord. Maybe my confession was my feeble attempt at intimacy, by opening up and being vulnerable with my new bride, but I think it was more about soothing my guilt. I felt better after getting it off my chest … but I dumped this pain on my young bride.

A few years into our marriage, I started traveling for work. I was alone, in a strange town, drinking—the perfect storm for having an affair—and I succumbed to temptation. I continued to live a double life, both lives void of true intimacy. I was not open or transparent, and my true self was all caught up in a drive I couldn't control.

One night Eldeen came to me to ask me to forgive her for what she was doing wrong in our marriage. The idea surprised me. It didn't seem to me like she was doing anything wrong. Then my thoughts went immediately to *Uh oh, she knows. She's trying to get me to admit what I'm doing wrong and lower a guillotine over my head.* But she wasn't out to get me at all. Instead, she asked me to forgive her for her unforgiveness and her anger.

Her confession overwhelmed me with guilt. I was so afraid of being known—really known. So I covered up my guilt with anger. I shook my head as I lashed back at her. "Eldeen, you don't know what you're talking about! I am living in the real world." I couldn't keep it in any longer, and I told Eldeen I had been cheating on her.

## Facing The Truth

*Eldeen*

I had suspected it. But still, I was not prepared for the truth. I am so glad Gene had not confessed two days earlier, because I would have walked out if he had. But I didn't. I couldn't. God had told me to stay.

I had always been independent. My parents owned two grocery stores, which came with heavy responsibilities. They coped with the heavy load with heavy drinking. So I was used to managing life on my own ... until I was pregnant, worried I was married to an alcoholic, thinking my life was over. I became suicidal, thoughts of the car spinning out of control as I drove down the road. I had worked and saved to buy my own car, a Volkswagen. But then, Gene got drunk and crashed it. He hadn't been drinking as much while we were dating because he'd been training for football. Then, as newlyweds and after football season ended, he drank heavily with his fraternity brothers, leaving me at home alone, pregnant, for hours on end.

Later, after he started his job, some nights I'd wake up at two or three in the morning and Gene still wasn't home, arriving home around four o'clock. I became so angry at his selfishness for leaving me to deal with the babies alone. I'd be so angry that he was so thoughtless. It was heartbreaking to me to see my life as it was unfolding.

Instead of intimacy, there was friction between us. I wanted my marriage to be so much more than it was. Those touch points—Gene looking up instead of at me as I walked down the aisle, seeing another woman during our engagement and confessing it the first night of our honeymoon, not being ready for our first child, Gene's excessive drinking and late nights—all brought layers of unforgiveness and bitterness. I had a foundation in my belief system that you don't get a divorce unless there's adultery. I felt trapped. I didn't know at the time that Gene was having affairs with other women. But I have to admit I suspected it. I got angrier and angrier because he was telling me lies. Lies provoke the person you're lying to, and anger is a result even though they don't know why. I was believing the lies, but our relationship was off, damaged.

Two nights before Gene's confession, I picked up a book and started reading. Gene was out of town on business and the children were asleep. I stayed up late reading *Beyond Ourselves* by Catherine Marshall. My life changed that evening.

The words quickly began to prick my mind and pierce my heart. Growing up, I went to church with my family. It was just something you did. I had no idea it was possible to know Jesus Christ in a personal way. As I continued to pour through the book, all of the things I had heard in church were now making sense. I realized what was missing from my life—intimacy— and that it could only be met in my marriage if it was met with God first. I didn't have that kind of intimacy with God up to that point. I had to grapple with and finally understand that my Christianity was formal, based on intellect. I had knowledge of God but not a heart experience with Him. That night, I said "I do" to Jesus, and I finally began to understand who He is, that He could do for me what nobody else could do—not even Gene. God is the only one who could fill my empty heart. This was the first time I began to understand intimacy.

I became acutely aware of the bitterness I harbored against Gene, all the way back to our honeymoon when he told me about seeing the girl in the inappropriate dress. Unforgiveness had started piling up from that point on.

After reading *Beyond Ourselves* that evening, I realized how much Christ loved me, and I was set free. God opened my eyes to intimacy with Him first and foremost. When you know you are forgiven and that He can forgive others through you, you don't need to carry the burden of unforgiveness anymore.

No matter what, I knew God wanted us to stay together. So I went to Gene to confess my unforgiveness and anger. I was able to say to Gene, "I can forgive you for anything you've ever done because I understand forgiveness through Christ."

That is why when Gene revealed the truth about his lifestyle, I was able to stay.

## A New Intimacy

Today, Eldeen and I are free to love and trust and enjoy each other to a depth we never knew could be possible. How did we get to this place of intimacy in our marriage after such pain and betrayal? I will tell you the rest of the story throughout the following chapters. What I can tell you now is that we walked through the pain, forgiveness, and healing together by the power and grace of our Lord. He gives us the ability to experience true intimacy—a deep, soul connection—as He had originally designed.

If you are feeling disconnected in your marriage, I understand. I know how painful unmet expectations and conditional love can be. I will always grieve the pain I caused my wife with my betrayal, witnessing firsthand the sorrow the lack of intimacy creates. Over the years, I've worked with numerous husbands and wives who have struggled to reclaim, or initiate, intimacy in their marriages. Thankfully, through God's wisdom and grace, I've witnessed restoration in many disconnected marriages that had seemed doomed to failure—including my own.

Take heart, my friend. God has a plan for intimacy for you in your situation as well. Stay with me as we explore His perfect plan for intimacy. He longs for you and your spouse to be a part of it.

CHAPTER 2

# A Perfect Union

T HE IDEA of meeting that one perfect man or woman, marrying, and living happily ever after did not originate in fairy tales. It goes back much farther than that—all the way back to the Garden of Eden. Our notions of intimacy, connection, finding our soulmate, and becoming one in marriage all stem from the days of creation. For a perfect image of untainted intimacy, we will have to go back to where all was perfect.

God has been about the business of creating. First the heavens, then the earth. Next came the oceans and the dry land. Then God filled the earth with all kinds of vegetation, followed by the sun, moon, and stars. It was not long before God made creatures to fill the ocean, sky, and land. And it was all good. But God was not done yet. "Then the LORD God formed a man from the dust of the ground and breathed into his nostrils the breath of life, and the man became a living being. Now the LORD God had planted a garden in the east, in Eden; and there he put the man he had formed" (Genesis 2:7–8).

Even before Adam had a chance to take in the sights, God knew it was not good for him to be alone. So He brought every creature before Adam to be named. Have you ever wondered why God put on this animal parade? Was it to see if any of these creatures would "fit the bill" as a companion for Adam? Not at all. God had planned from the very beginning to create woman—man's perfect mate. The task of reviewing the animals was for Adam's benefit. It was all part of his preparation for an intimate relationship with a female human being. The first man was about to get the gift of a lifetime, and he needed to be ready for it. He needed to see what he was missing by not having a mate of his own.

## Boy Meets Girl

By the time Adam finished naming the animals, he had become keenly aware of a longing in himself that could not be satisfied. Nothing in creation connected with him on his human level. The whole basis for intimacy is a human relationship that God created. When God created the first human, Adam had no one to communicate with at the five-sense level. Adam communicated with God in perfect spirit and truth but not through the five senses God created him with. There was no one to connect with through those senses until Eve was born. So God did some surgery on Adam … and created woman.

The man said,
"This is now bone of my bones
and flesh of my flesh;
she shall be called 'woman,'
for she was taken out of man."
That is why a man leaves his father and mother
and is united to his wife, and they become one
flesh. (Genesis 2:23–24)

In their perfect union, something was born that would be inherited by all mankind: the desire to love and be loved in return. You could say Adam and Eve celebrated the first marriage.

Mike Mason describes this beautifully in his book, *The Mystery of Marriage*:

When Eve came into the world, she was not simply Eve; she was all human relationship. She was formed out of the very body of Adam, born out of him in order that she might enjoy an especially close bond with him, a bond which was not only to be the cornerstone of all future relations between people on Earth, but which was to be the definition of humanity: "Male and female He created them" (Genesis 1:27). So special a thing was this in God's eyes that He saved it until last, until all the rest of His creative work was in place. The making of Eve was a sort of "up-level," a second stage added onto creation with a view to reproducing in the human race a reflection of God's own multi-personhood. Man was not to be an isolated creature, nor a whole horde of isolated creatures, but rather "one flesh," an entity somehow composite yet with no loss of individuality, united but without forfeiting the stupendous beauty and mystery of otherness: not man alone, but mankind.

Adam was a man alone, a singleton. But in the company of Eve, he became a race, a corporate body, and only then did he become capable of mirroring the true and full life of God, which is the life of loving relationship ...[3]

So in the beginning, everything was perfect. God created man and woman and placed them in the Garden of Eden. In its perfection, the Garden was a safe place—safe from sin, condemnation, rejection, fights, misunderstandings—everything was safe. Even the animals were safe because they felt no threat from man. There was absolutely no danger anywhere, no crime, no abuse, no disease. There was not one natural disaster. You name it—whatever was not safe was not there.

In this safe place, Adam and Eve felt safe to be themselves. They could safely express their thoughts and feelings. They were safe to be vulnerable and transparent to the very core of their being, without any fear. They were totally naked—mentally, emotionally, and physically. This was pure intimacy.

In his book *When Men Think Private Thoughts*, Gordon MacDonald describes the pure intimacy between Adam and Eve: "Here nakedness has to do not only with an unclothed body but also with an unclothed soul. If the soul is understood to be the deepest depths of the human being, then nakedness suggests two people who are totally open to each other. No secrets!"[4]

Think of your marriage for a moment. Can you honestly claim you have never kept any secrets from your spouse? No secrets at all, no matter how big or small. No hidden shame, no self-protection. It is hard to picture, isn't it? I have to confess, as you already know, I kept lots of secrets from Eldeen … until I finally surrendered my heart fully to God. Just as gaining intimacy is a process, so was my letting go of my control and trusting God.

### Guilty Until ...

Sometimes I would confess to Eldeen about little things just to get her off my back. But this time was different. I opened up and admitted to her I had been unfaithful. The next two and a half years after my confession were a living hell for Eldeen. We moved to a new city where she was alone except for me and our girls. And I did not help. I did whatever I wanted, whenever I wanted. That mindset continued to put me in temptation's way. My personality opens up quickly, a quality I discovered attracted women to me. Looking back now, I can see how my unguarded strength of openness left me vulnerable. I tell my clients often: Unguarded strength becomes a double weakness. Double because you are not guarding your strength and you are letting someone else take advantage of your strength. That's where I was. As a result, there was no intimacy in our marriage relationship. All I did was cause Eldeen more pain. I was determined to be the master of my own life.

*Unguarded strength becomes a double weakness—you are not guarding your strength and you are letting someone else take advantage of your strength.*

I think I became more determined the more Eldeen trusted God. I could not deny that in the midst of our horrible marriage, she was faithful to what God told her. The love and forgiveness of God was so evident in her life during that time.

At one point, Eldeen came home from a Campus Crusade for Christ (now called Cru) seminar at church. She was excited about a booklet called *The Four Spiritual Laws*.[5] In the few minutes she shared it with me, the truth of the gospel hit me. It was not enough to know the facts about God, it stated. We are to invite God into our lives and put Him on the throne of our lives. In other words, give Him control. That truth stopped me short. I was terrified of giving God control of my life because I thought He would get me back for all I was doing. My fear blocked me from intimacy with God and intimacy with Eldeen.

I was trying to make my life right. I tried to love Eldeen in my own strength. But the more I tried, the more I failed, and the more miserable I became. I could not make myself right and I could not love my wife the way a husband is supposed to. No matter how hard I tried, I could not stop cheating on Eldeen. I knew I was wrong. I tried to change in my own power to stop having sex with other women. I'd achieve it for a while and then I'd give in again. And still, when Eldeen showed me the four circles about control in *The Four Spiritual Laws* booklet, I got mad. I didn't want to give up control.

I believe this is true for so many of us. We don't give up control to God because we don't trust He has our best interest in mind. That's a direct link to marriage. We can trust our spouse if we know he or she has our best interest at the forefront of their mind. How could I have Eldeen's best interest in mind if I kept betraying her? That truth exposed the reality of pain my double life caused my wife and the grief it caused me, yet I didn't have the strength to change. I tried. I tried to change in my own power and I failed.

Not long after Eldeen shared *The Four Spiritual*

> We don't give up control to God because we don't trust He has our best interest in mind. That's a direct link to marriage. We can trust our spouse if we know he or she has our best interest at the forefront of their mind.

*Laws* with me, I attended a sales manager meeting in Chicago. It turns out we ended up playing a psychological game that challenged our abilities and beliefs about trust. At the time, our company was getting ready to lay off several employees. After the so-called "game," I went to my sales manager, a good Italian Catholic, and got in his face. "What's this blankety-blank about trust?! If it's my job or yours, guess who's going?" I spit out the word "trust!" in anger as I walked away.

I was being convicted about my trust issue … only I didn't know it. I went back to my hotel room to pull myself together. A few moments later, after I'd simmered down a bit, I heard a still, small voice in the quietness of the room.

"You're a phony."

The truth hit me hard. God brought me face-to-face with the truth about myself: I *was* a phony. *And I knew it.* He showed me I didn't truly love anybody. I didn't trust anybody. I was so frustrated and angry with myself. In the quietness of my hotel room late that night, I gave up.

"Okay, Lord," I cried. "I quit. Come into my life and take control. Do whatever you want to do."

God had used a team-building game about trust among my colleagues in the middle of Chicago at the Water Tower Inn to show me why our marriage lacked intimacy. I didn't trust anybody, not even my wife. And because of my double life, she couldn't trust me. Even though she was my wife, she didn't feel completely loved by me. I was a phony. No wonder my marriage was in such trouble. Trust is a key element to intimacy. My life started to change from that point on. And so did our marriage.

Achieving pure, constant intimacy is a work in progress for each one of us. We might taste the connectedness of intimacy for a time, then life happens. A conflict occurs or a disagreement causes pain, and we pull back or lash out, losing touch with the intimacy we'd been enjoying. I don't want to mislead you. None of us can stay in a constant state of perfect intimacy with our marriage partner. No couple reaches full perfection in their intimacy with each other 100 percent of the time. We live in a broken world where perfection doesn't exist. However, we can each work toward having more intimacy with our spouse than we've ever had before. Working toward authentic intimacy in marriage is a process and one well worth the effort.

*Achieving pure, constant intimacy is a work in progress for each one of us. We might taste the connectedness of intimacy for a time, then life happens. A conflict occurs or a disagreement causes pain, and we pull back or lash out, losing touch with the intimacy we'd been enjoying.*

While we can only dream of perfection, Adam and Eve lived it. The connection they had with God was perfect, unhindered—an unbroken communion. The connection they had with each other was also perfect. In both cases—with God and with each other—Adam and Eve experienced true intimacy. While Adam and Eve always retained their individuality and uniqueness, they shared a comingling of their entire beings with each other. It is hard for us to grasp this original intimacy.

The first man and woman were totally committed to relating with the other for their best, with noble motives. They shared a common mission in life. It also appears they appreciated each other's personhood. You can envision them simply enjoying being together in the garden. On top of all that, they experienced no shame or guilt. No offense, no irritation, with each other or with God. There was no embarrassment or fear of being discovered a fraud. Each could present his or her soul to the other without fear of condemnation.

That was God's design for mankind: perfect intimacy in marriage.

Then with one act of disobedience, God's perfect design was destroyed and relationships became unsafe. When Adam and Eve chose to disobey God and eat from the one forbidden tree in the Garden of Eden, everything changed. Where it once was safe to be totally known before the Lord, Adam was now afraid. So he hid. Where it once was safe to be totally naked before his wife, man was now ashamed. So he clothed himself. The same was true for Eve.

> Then the eyes of both of them were opened, and
> they realized they were naked; so they sewed fig
> leaves together and made coverings for themselves.

Then the man and his wife heard the sound of the LORD God as he was walking in the garden in the cool of the day, and they hid from the LORD God among the trees of the garden. But the LORD God called to the man, "Where are you?"

He answered, "I heard you in the garden, and I was afraid because I was naked; so I hid."

And he said, "Who told you that you were naked? Have you eaten from the tree that I commanded you not to eat from?" (Genesis 3:7–11)

God knew where they were. He also knew the guilt and shame, the loss of intimacy, they were dealing with.

The whole picture in the Garden of Eden changed in an instant. Everything was affected. The ramifications of the Fall transformed man, the animal kingdom, and even the environment. A brand-new emotion entered into the heart of man—*fear*. Man was now afraid. He was afraid of the beasts, afraid of growing food. Most of all, he was afraid of facing God's perfection. Afraid of being in the presence of the One who loved him the most … the very One who had created him … the One who knew him. The connection between God and man was broken.

From that point on, Adam and Eve also became afraid of one another, afraid of interacting with the only other human being in existence. Afraid of undressing and being naked with one another. Afraid of emotionally undressing and being transparent. Afraid to pursue one another to the deepest part of their being. Afraid of the imperfections they now saw within themselves and in each other. The connection between man and woman was broken as well as the connection with God.

## Bridge to Intimacy

The perfect communion that Adam and Eve shared with each other and with God was gone. In its place was a chasm that I would imagine felt as huge as the Grand Canyon. Each of us has inherited that same gap. This is what is meant by the phrase "being born in Adam." Our humanness in our fallen world is known as our "flesh." The word "flesh" is described as "the body, especially as distinguished from the spirit or soul."[6] As in, "The spirit is willing, but the flesh is weak" (Matthew 26:41). "Flesh" is also described as "the physical or animal nature." As human beings we have all three—spirit and soul along with our "flesh." So when I refer to our "flesh," I am referring to our physical, animal nature. As we seek to connect, to experience true intimacy, not only do we need to deal with the spiritual gap we are born with but also the nature of our "flesh."

It is critical to recognize we live in a fallen, broken world. We learn to fear intimacy from the get-go because of the Fall. Nobody comes into the world trusting their Heavenly Father, much less another human being. We find it difficult to place our trust in another person. Each of us has a longing to connect at a deep human level, yet we also have anxiety or fear of what's going to happen if we express what's going on inside of us. We don't speak up honestly out of fear of not receiving the response we would like. By nature, our inner self hides, blames others, and runs from self-exposure. We have a strong fear of being hurt. And yet, human beings have been created to totally experience intimacy. Just like Adam and Eve, who lost intimacy with their Creator, we each encounter that same gap with God because of the broken world we're born into.

I will give you the bad news first: There is nothing you can do about the gap in your life between you and God. We were born with fear because of the Fall. The good news: There is One who has already bridged that chasm. Jesus Christ paid the penalty for our disobedience (both inherited and of our own making), or sin. He, who knew no sin, took the condemnation of our sin on Himself. He has made it safe for us to enter into the presence of the Lord.

Yes, God designed us to experience intimacy with another human being, but He first designed us to be intimate with Him. Entering into a personal relationship with God through Jesus Christ reconnects us to God. And only then do we truly have the ability to connect, to bridge the gap, to another human being on a soul level. Through His power we can face our fears that separate us from the ones we really want to know. Just like Adam and Eve, if we hide anything from God, we're going to hide things from our spouse as well.

That's how it works. And the opposite is also true. Intimacy with your spouse all starts with your intimacy with Jesus. When you overcome the fear of being yourself with Him and learn to hide nothing from Him, you free yourself to be intimate with your spouse. Where there is freedom to be ourselves in relationships, there is a bridge to intimacy.

So the number one step to intimacy in your marriage is to pursue your relationship with the Lord Jesus and give Him control of your life. To have intimacy with another person flows from true intimacy with God. Only God's power can release us to experience pure, unadulterated intimacy, as it did in the beginning for the first couple, Adam and Eve.

*So the number one step to intimacy in your marriage is to pursue your relationship with the Lord Jesus and give Him control of your life. To have intimacy with another person flows from true intimacy with God.*

## CHAPTER 3

# The Way God Designed It

P EOPLE COME to see me when they are absolutely desperate, their marriages in the "valley of the shadow of death." They feel hurt, angry, bitter, and hopeless. I have worked with many couples who feared their marriage was beyond hope, the gap too wide, the connection of intimacy all but dissolved. They come to me as a last resort. Frequently when couples first come to see me, they ask, "What do you think? Is there hope? Will our marriage make it?"

I have the same answer for everyone.

"I am not God; I cannot control what happens. What we can control is what we do this moment. Let us just go through this process and trust God. We'll leave the end result in His hands." I have learned to not judge a marriage as it appears to be; rather, I try to see it as what it could be when both partners unreservedly give themselves to Christ. And that takes time.

A common statement I hear is: "If this doesn't work, it's all over."

Will and Melanie were in that exact spot. Both were Christians, but each had drifted away from God.

Then Will's life was completely torn apart when he learned Melanie was having an affair. "Our marriage was at death's doorstep. As far as I was concerned, there wasn't a whole lot left," Will said. Still very much in love with Melanie, Will wanted to save their marriage, not only for both of them but for their two young children as well.

But Melanie was not interested at all. In fact, she had already left the marriage, mentally and emotionally. Melanie said, "I know I was very far from God, and in my marriage I was already gone mentally, so all I had left was to pack my bags. I was ready to leave and get on with my life somewhere else." Melanie thought Will would gladly watch her leave when she told him the truth about the affair. Surely, he would not want her anymore and would kick her out.

However, Will refused to believe the marriage might be over. "I was heartbroken at the time. I was afraid of losing Melanie, especially since she was willing to abandon the children. All I could think about was racing toward God." So, Will frantically searched the Scriptures and came across this verse: "Therefore, I say unto you, Whatever things you desire, when you pray, believe that you receive them, and you shall have them" (Mark 11:24, KJV). He also studied the book of Hosea about the prophet's own wife's betrayal in their marriage that was eventually restored by God.

And that's exactly what Will did.

Will began spending time with God, reading the Bible, and praying for a miracle. Still hurt by Melanie's betrayal and her desire to get out of the marriage, Will pursued God more than ever. Once Will took a fair and unbiased assessment of himself, he was shocked to find how much room there was for improvement in his own behavior. Further, he discovered this verse: "And be not conformed to this world, but be ye transformed by the renewing of your mind" (Romans 12:2 KJV).

Will asked Melanie to stay and go to counseling. Reluctantly, Melanie agreed. "I did not share the hope Will had that our marriage could be saved. But he did not kick me out. In fact, he did exactly the opposite of what I expected. Somewhere in the deepest depths of my heart, I felt like this was my last chance to really be helped."

When Will and Melanie first came into my office, I must admit I had not known two people to be at such opposite ends of the spectrum. As desperately as Will wanted to hang on to Melanie, she was just as desperate to get out of the marriage. Melanie was severely depressed and somewhat suicidal. Opposite of Melanie, Will was resolutely clinging to God, believing Him for the impossible.

I run into this paradox constantly with clients on the path to healing. While Melanie was the one who had an affair, Will was the one who needed to change first. When you have been betrayed, it is extremely difficult not to focus on the shortcomings of the other person, but Will had to stop looking at what Melanie had done wrong and focus on what he had been doing wrong.

From my experience as a therapist, I understood Will needed to know what was coming in the counseling process. And because Will was seeking God, asking for direction on how to make changes in his own life, he was ready to hear what I told him next.

"Will, you are going to have do something that will cause you more pain. You are going to have to risk being so vulnerable that it is going to scare you half to death. I can tell you this: You're not going to want to do it."

Will couldn't believe there could possibly be more pain than what he was already experiencing, but he had only scratched the surface of his pain. Even though I had hit Will with the truth of what lay ahead, I encouraged him not to give up hope. Before he collapsed out of fear from what I would have him do, I explained what he would gain. He would experience an emotional intimacy and a "connectedness" so deep—completely without the physical—it would blow his mind.

I explained to Will that the revelation of Melanie's affair was a symptom of much deeper problems. We would have to work through Melanie's issues slowly, unraveling the wrong thinking and the lies from her background that led her into the bondage of destructive behavioral patterns. We would also need to confront the lies Will had lived under for years. Thankfully, God through the Holy Spirit can work in situations that seem impossible. Will was willing to believe me and began to open up.

## Creating a Safe Place

At the beginning of counseling, I told Will to prepare for the worst. I also told him to pursue Melanie if he wanted her back. Pray for her. All of this is especially hard to do when you have been hurt through betrayal. In spite of the other person's reactions, you must pursue what God wants you to do, in the sufficiency of His grace.

"After I learned that," Will said, "I made Melanie the focus of everything I did. I made a list of her likes and dislikes. I thought up things to do on dates. I took her on trips. I wrote her poetry. I did everything I could to love her. I did my best and knew I had the sufficiency of God's grace to take care of the rest."

I knew the next couple of months would be difficult and frightening for them both, so the counseling room needed to be a safe place. Melanie was not ready to let go of her fear of intimacy, of getting close. Her programming ran deep. So I put the responsibility on Will to take the lead. Emotionally skittish at first, Melanie was confused by Will's response to her. He did not reject her but kept on loving her, more than he ever had.

She knew she had Will's support. Now it was my turn.

I deal with each person I counsel at a different speed, so to speak. My motto is: "Truth is never optional; timing and method are." I must bring people to the truth, but I do that when they are ready to handle it appropriately. Due to Melanie's fragile state, I handled her delicately. Although she was the one who had committed the sin of adultery, I did not exhort her.

Her trust in me grew when she realized I was not going to condemn her. Most Christians who have sinned believe they will be condemned with the truth. I wanted to help Melanie see that the truth would set her free. I did not want to condemn or reject her with it. Slowly, Melanie began to believe I had her best interest in mind.

My goal was to create an environment through God's power and guidance where Melanie and Will could be free to be themselves in each other's presence—the definition of true intimacy. In order to peel away the layers of hurt and protection to express their deep thoughts and feelings, they had to feel it was safe. I do not ask people to trust each other right away. It is ludicrous to tell a person they need to trust someone who has just betrayed them. I do ask them to work on building an environment of respect where each can learn to share their feelings in safety. This was set up in my office, and I wanted it in their home also. Therefore, I suggested they not separate.

Often, couples in similar situations ask me if they should separate. Most of the time I don't think it's wise. Separation gives people a psychological peace, but they never fully deal with their issues. It is always tougher to stay and face the lies and the pain than it is to leave. There are times when it is better to separate, especially when there is violence, but I didn't see that with Will and Melanie.

Looking back, they both saw the wisdom in not separating. Will said, "When you are separated, you do not confront. We had to learn how to confront each issue as mature adults. If either of us did something the other didn't like, we had to dig through all of the symptoms before we actually got to the root cause. We had to learn to do that. Sometimes our 'sessions' lasted two to three hours before we got to the root cause. Then it began taking us less time to reach the real issue."

The control issue was tough for Will. Admittedly, he said, "I am a control person. I had to learn to give control over to God and focus on myself. I had to change. All this time I wanted Melanie to change, but I discovered that God wanted me to work on myself and to give Him the rest; He would take care of it all."

People talk about "becoming like Christ." I say, *let Christ live His life in and through you.* You don't produce Christ. He lives His presence in you. You give Him control of your life to produce intimacy with your spouse. He fills us with the capacity for intimacy. Will experienced this as he continued in his personal relationship with Jesus.

## Patterns from Childhood

Melanie began to recall some experiences that were very painful to her. "When I was two years old, my mother abused me mentally. She would scream at the top of her lungs, throw my toys, and slam doors. She was angry at my father, but I didn't know that at the time."

Melanie felt so much pain in remembering the angry outbursts of her mother. Now she had some answers as to why she always felt so unloved and unprotected. These feelings were only amplified when her parents divorced. As a result, she couldn't believe someone would have her best interest in mind. Her innate fear of intimacy (that we are all born with) was only validated in these experiences.

Will and Melanie each grew up seeing betrayal from both parents. In Melanie's situation, her father left her mother when Melanie was a teenager. She said, "I think they both betrayed each other, but my father physically left. My mother then withdrew. Besides my sister, I did not have anyone else in my life. I had to depend completely on myself, but then I also became my mother's emotional caretaker."

Will recalled his childhood this way: "My dad would betray my mom by withdrawing from her, choosing not to be emotionally involved with her. My mom would then betray him by ridiculing him to us kids. Betrayal was going both ways. I repeated Mom and Dad's pattern in my marriage to Melanie. I was not intimate with her mentally, emotionally, or spiritually. Based on the example set by my parents, I didn't know how to be truly intimate with my own wife."

Melanie developed a pattern of shiftlessness: "After my father left, my mother intimated that I should have shallow physical relationships and then leave. She was so bitter toward my father; I think she passed this bitterness on to me. When it came to men, I thought it was okay to be involved but not get married or have anything serious—just have a meaningless relationship, then leave. By doing that there would be no mental or emotional anguish once the relationship was over. This became my pattern."

Once this pattern was set in place, Melanie never totally gave herself to any relationship. She would get involved and get her needs met to a certain point, then she would back out. This continued into her marriage, leading to the vulnerability to have an affair.

Eventually, it became safer to Melanie outside the marriage than in it. When Will would wall himself off emotionally from Melanie, she was hurt and sought someone else to meet her needs. Melanie only found a false or counterfeit intimacy in the extramarital relationships. The deception in affairs is that the unfaithful partner believes they can be more themselves with the other person than with their own spouse. Confronting this lie is difficult because when a person is entrapped in this pattern, the counterfeit intimacy feels real. In truth, the potential to be totally intimate is within marriage, the way God designed it.

By the time they came to see me, Melanie did not want Will to touch her. He felt painfully rejected. Often our concept of what we need each other for is distorted. A man thinks that if his wife does not give herself to him, he is going to die. (Believe me, women; this is how many a man thinks.)

In reality, although we need sex, the most important thing a man needs from his wife is letting her inside of him emotionally. To be known in this way, a man needs to be emotionally vulnerable to his wife.

There is nothing scarier to a man.

A man's strength is his physicality. He feels most a man when he is physically connected to his wife. A woman feels more like a woman than at any other time when she is emotionally connected with her man. This is a woman's strength. And this is what strikes fear in a man.

Will admits, "I had never let Melanie know me before. The thought of it filled me with pure fear. If I let her know me and it's not good for her, then I am rejected even more." In spite of his fears, Will trusted God, believed truth, and began to let Melanie in emotionally.

With time, Will and Melanie told me about an experience they had on a flight to a friend's wedding in a different state. They began sharing their thoughts and feelings with each other. In a moment, they experienced an incredible emotional connection. They felt closer than they ever had in their lives. Laughingly, Will said it was just his luck they were on an airplane surrounded by people.

When you connect emotionally, the physical will take care of itself. In some cases, it just takes a little time. Will backed off from a physical relationship until Melanie was ready. The more Melanie felt an emotional connection with Will, the more willing she was to let go physically. Will took his cues from his wife. At first, Melanie was only comfortable with a little hug, then she was able to move on to holding hands. Will never forced her into something she was not comfortable with. As he gave Melanie time and space, her physical feelings returned. Even more beautiful, as Will and Melanie intimately opened their hearts to Jesus and one another, their physical intimacy with one another grew exponentially.

## Putting "Un" in Conditional Love

All of us learn to love conditionally. Based on certain conditions, we will allow ourselves to love only if we deem the other person worthy of our devotion. We look for qualities that match our evaluation of what's most important and we shower our love on that person, but only as long as they meet our standard. One misstep and our commitment to love is threatened.

On top of that, we tend to set up conditions to receive love as well. It is the old if/then scenario. If this good thing happens, or if that bad thing does not happen, then it is perceived as love. For example, as long as the wife does his bidding and agrees to snuggle in bed, the husband feels loved. As long as the husband showers his wife with positive accolades, she feels loved. And on the contrary, if she looks at him in a certain way, he feels unloved. Or if he uses a certain tone with her, she is certain he no longer loves her.

Unfortunately, many of us have no idea of the conditions we place on giving and getting love. We just know we feel unloved when the conditions are not met. Melanie did not feel loved or lovable due to the conditioning of her childhood. She couldn't imagine a husband who remained faithful to her in light of her behavior. Without the unconditional love of God, Will would not have been able to stay in the marriage with such a loving heart.

In looking back on the recovery process, Will now says, "Throughout this whole time, God loved me and was involved in everything that was going on. In the midst of all the tragedy, I had such a thread of joy. It was unmistakably the hand of God." Will later said, "It is a true statement that happiness is a choice, but joy comes from the Lord." God had shown Will His *agape* love—His unconditional love—and had given Will the strength to love Melanie the same way.

In many ways, I could relate to Melanie. I had been resisting giving up control for years. I had the intensity of a linebacker. As Eldeen says, linebackers are tough. And the tougher you are, the harder it is to surrender. Yet, like Melanie, deep down I wanted to be helped.

My marriage with Eldeen started to be restored when I finally opened the door to Jesus that night in Chicago.

### Eldeen

I knew immediately when he called me. His voice was different. It was obvious that Christ had become real to Gene during that trip to Chicago. After Gene returned home, I started to see changes in him. There was a softness to him now, a new openness. I now saw the tenderness I always knew was there, even though it had become so hard. Here was the man I thought I had married. And more.

After I surrendered my life to God that night at the Water Tower Inn, I didn't feel anything different and went to bed. The next morning, the Spirit of the living God came over me. I surprised myself when I turned down an invitation to have sex with another woman. We were caught in an elevator. What are the chances? It got stuck around the 40th floor, and she hinted at meeting later. But I had the power to say no.

I had the power to say no to the sin!

I could no longer say the Lord's name in vain. I started to see things I never saw before. I was being changed by no effort of my own except surrendering control to the Lord. I know not everyone has instant change like that, but God did that for me. He has His way of causing us to come around. Also, Eldeen's prayers and forgiveness held tremendous power as well.

### Eldeen

In that initial time of me coming to Christ, I kept praying and waiting and wrestling with God: Why isn't this man changing? Why am I having to put up with this behavior, which is totally outside of my belief system and my desire? But the Holy Spirit impressed in me to stay and to continue on.

Before Gene's surrender to Christ, when we disagreed or he had an emotional tirade about something insignificant because of his own guilt, I locked myself in the bathroom to get out of his way, to not respond. I sensed I was to be quiet and just pray and move on. After Gene became a Christian, I was released from the bathroom. I could speak what I was impressed to speak or, as the need arose, kick him.

I only did that once.

One morning it was time to move on and go to church, and Gene was acting like a child about being late. We had two little kids to get ready, and running late for Gene is oftentimes his norm. That time, after being set free from so long of not responding to his behavior, I gained my resolve and said with force, "This is not okay. We're going to church! Let's move on!" And my foot swung. I think it surprised us both. But Gene had said he wanted me to be more open with him, so I was. That's when we started seeing a change in our marriage. We became open. We made confessions to each other.

During that two and a half years that Eldeen was a Christian and I wasn't, she was trying to change me, and I was trying to change myself in my own way ... and it wasn't working. I couldn't stop sinning. I was trying. I couldn't deal with this problem because I didn't have a relationship with

Christ. Until I surrendered to Christ, I couldn't say no to sin.

And Eldeen's attempts to help me weren't helping because I was resisting her. I'd been wrestling against change with a 5'2", half-my-size person. After my wife stopped trying to change me, the wrestling match was between God and me, period.

So that evening after the trust-building game at the Water Tower Inn, with no other person in the room, I surrendered. I didn't yet have spiritual maturity, but I did see God working in my life almost immediately. After I surrendered to Christ, after I quit trying to change myself on my own, I started to live from the inside out rather than only from the outside. Over time I grew in spiritual maturity, which furthered my intimacy with Jesus and with Eldeen. The process to intimacy in our marriage required both of us to pursue intimacy with Christ. It took time for us both to reach that point.

Despite my continued unfaithfulness, Eldeen continued to pray for me. She opened up to me in vulnerability, asking my forgiveness for her anger. God empowered her to surrender the responsibility of my behavior to Him to deal with.

I have not met a person who does not want to be loved for who they are, just the way they are. That is unconditional love. When I confessed my unfaithfulness to Eldeen, I was not worthy of her devotion. I had broken our marriage vows. Yet she chose to forgive me and love me unconditionally. She loved me despite my weakness and betrayal. As she grew in her relationship with her Heavenly Father, she was able to love me with His love. God's love changed both our lives.

We see evidence of God's unconditional love throughout the Bible.

> But God is so rich in mercy, and he loved us so much, that even though we were dead because of our sins, he gave us life when he raised Christ from the dead. (It is only by God's grace that you have been saved!) For he raised us from the dead along with Christ and seated us with him in the heavenly realms because we are united with Christ Jesus. So God can point to us in all future ages as examples of the incredible wealth of his grace and kindness toward us, as shown in all he has done for us who are united with Christ Jesus. (Ephesians 2:4–7, NLT)

> This is how God showed his love among us: He sent his one and only Son into the world that we might live through him. This is love: not that we loved God, but that he loved us and sent his Son as an atoning sacrifice for our sins. (1 John 4:9–10)

> And hope does not put us to shame, because God's love has been poured out into our hearts through the Holy Spirit, who has been given to us.
> You see, at just the right time, when we were still powerless, Christ died for the ungodly. Very

rarely will anyone die for a righteous person, though for a good person someone might possibly dare to die. But God demonstrates his own love for us in this: While we were still sinners, Christ died for us. (Romans 5:5–8)

These are powerful professions of God's unconditional love for us, His unworthy people. And still … Christians come to me all the time with the same issue: "I know in my head that God loves me unconditionally. I can recite the verses. I have memorized the words. Then why do I not sense that love? Why do I not experience it?"

The conditions we have set up (whether we're aware of them or not) to give and receive love and the mechanisms we use for protection actually block us from experiencing the unconditional love of God and others. We will look more closely at these defense mechanisms in Chapter 9. But for now, I want to point out that only when we give up the conditions that have become so familiar, so rooted, can we receive His love. And only then will we be able to love others intimately, unconditionally, the way He loves us. The way He designed us.

Every situation is different, but many marriages come to the point of believing they have no hope. They begin to believe it is better to split up. They buy into the mindset of "I cannot see how God would want me to stay in this situation the rest of my life." All hope is gone.

But at the point of absolute helplessness and hopelessness you meet the God of hope. In His grace, you can experience the true meaning of intimacy. God designed you to have intimacy with Him and with your spouse. He designed you to live in forgiveness. He designed you to trust Him, to surrender your control to His divine love, and to walk through your life in humble transparency within your marriage. The God of hope offers His power to you to have intimacy in your marriage—as He designed it.

*At the point of absolute helplessness and hopelessness you meet the God of hope. In His grace, you can experience the true meaning of intimacy. God designed you to have intimacy with Him and with your spouse.*

CHAPTER 4

# The Power of Image

A DAM AND Eve had a lot going for them. Besides being perfect, they had unblemished, crystal-clear self-images. They understood the untarnished pictures of the male and female image. They knew who they were, independently and together—man and woman were created in God's perfect image.

"So God created mankind in his own image, in the image of God he created them; male and female he created them" (Genesis 1:27).

As human beings, we were created in God's character. We were created:

- with dignity. (Genesis 1:26–27)
- with authority. (vs. 26)
- to receive a blessing and provision. (vs. 28–29)
- with purpose and meaning. (Genesis 2:15–19)
- with a sense of freedom and boundary. (vs. 16–17)
- to have love and intimate companionship. (vs. 20–25)

Before the Fall, everything in creation was in perfect alignment with its Creator. Man and woman were secure in who they were created to be. As Adam and Eve interacted with each other and their environment, all the information they gathered through their senses was true. There was nothing to distort the truth. Everything they saw, tasted, smelled, heard, and felt was true.

Then the Fall threw everything out of whack.

What does that mean for us? Since we are born into a broken world, our senses are not controlled by God but by the things in this world. As children, we learn to distinguish right from wrong, and we train our senses through what we experience. This means we cannot trust that the information we gather from our senses is necessarily true. That includes the image we hold of ourselves.

## Limited Vision

In my therapy practice, I frequently see people who are not in touch with what's going on inside of them. Nobody's perfect at that, but inner awareness is an important prerequisite to intimacy. Besides knowing what we feel or what we're experiencing at the moment, we need to be able to know who we are, what we are here for, and where we are going. When I ask somebody the question, "Who are you?" they oftentimes look blank, not knowing how to answer. So I'll

*There are three things that make up who you are: hard wiring, experience, and how God sees you.*

repeat, "Who are you? How do you define who you are?" And it makes people think. How can you be intimate if you don't even know who you are?

Consider these three questions for yourself:

> Who am I?
> What am I here for?
> Where am I going?

These are important questions for us to answer as we examine our self-image.

There are three things that make up who you are: hard wiring, experience, and how God sees you. Let's look at each of these more closely.

1. Hard wiring from the womb.

While writing this book, Eldeen and I became great-grandparents for the first time. Our tiny newborn great-granddaughter already has her very own personality that was created in her mother's womb. Nobody else on earth will be like her. There's something incredibly personal about that.

Each of us is born with a unique personality. As a result, we have a filter within us that causes us to see things differently in some degree than anybody else. And I think that's special and unique. There's nobody else like you. That means nobody else sees you as you see yourself. You have thoughts that are private to you. You have your own way of reasoning, your brain's specific way of processing information, your internal dialogue. As you were "knit together" in your mother's womb, your brain started developing its own connections. You are uniquely you.

2. Life's experiences.

The conditions we grow up with, combined with the experiences we have throughout our life, further shape our self-image. We absorb a tremendous amount of self-worth and identity through our home environment. (We'll go into this in more detail in Part Two.) As we mature, we develop a lot of who we are through what happens to us. Our feelings, our emotions, are hooked up to our senses. Keep in mind … your senses are trained in this broken world. You may sense, think, or feel something that got generated in this broken world that isn't really true about you. Throughout our life experience, we become keenly aware of how other people see us. Our self-image often reflects how we believe other people see us based on our actions, rather than who we really are inside.

And then you go through more life experiences, and the more you're in a relationship with the opposite sex and marriage, the more you begin to battle with how you see yourself through their eyes. We assign who we are based upon what we know from our experiences. The world's system tells us performance plus appearance brings approval. That's not God's formula. God goes to the heart.

3. How God sees you.

When we are born into this broken world, our identity is not in Christ because we don't yet have the Spirit of God in us. We can't see ourselves the way God sees us until we are in personal relationship with Him. So our identity is formed from what we experience around us, how other people treat us, how people didn't treat us. All of those experiences are contained in our brain. We never forget anything, although we aren't able to recall everything, and these thoughts shape our beliefs about ourselves.

But here is the beautiful truth: God sees you as His beloved child, His workmanship, created for good works, chosen, wonderfully made, a dwelling place for His Spirit.[7] The Scripture is full of Christ's words saying, "Here's how I see you. Here's who you are." He knows you intimately and values you just as you are.[8] The ultimate goal is for us to see ourselves as our Heavenly Father sees us.

By ourselves, we can only see our self-image with limited vision. We see ourselves through our experiences and through the eyes of other people. No one comes into the world seeing themselves through God's eyes, even though He sees us the most accurately. We don't have the capacity to see ourselves how God sees us until we accept Christ and the Spirit of God enters our heart and mind. We hold expectations of ourselves that, if unmet, cause us to take on a sense of disappointment in ourselves that is hard to shake.

My self-image had been wrapped up in football. While Eldeen was pregnant with our first child, I tried out with the Denver Broncos—and pulled a hamstring. They told me to go home and heal, then play for a year with a semi-pro team in Boston before I could try out again for the NFL. I wasn't willing to do that. It was tough for me to give up my dream of pro football. So much of my identity was wrapped up in it. But I don't know what would have happened to our marriage if I'd gone on to play with the Broncos. I believe God's sovereignty protected me. He spared me from a potentially broken body from a football career as well as the seemingly unlimited availability and temptation of women.

Getting your needs met outside of God's way develops an image of yourself, but it also distorts who you are. I struggled with the image I was portraying as well as the image I had of myself. I tried to stop myself from sinning, but I couldn't do it on my own. I couldn't stop, and that's what brought me to my knees in surrender to Christ. By the time I finally threw in the towel, my self-image was messed up. I could name who I was based on my activities in this world, as an athlete and a football player. But deep down in my soul, I didn't even know who I was.

Underlying everything in me was a feeling of inadequacy. There was a part of me that was trying to prove I was a man by conquering women. Looking back now, I can see how the image I had of myself was so distorted. And each encounter with another woman worked only to further distort and destroy my true image. My self-image finally began to be restored as I entered into an intimate relationship with God. But it didn't happen overnight.

As I started growing in spiritual maturity and intimacy with Christ, Eldeen started treating me differently. Eldeen learned early in her relationship with Jesus that she couldn't fix me.

### Eldeen

When I'm asked if I had any doubts that Gene might be unfaithful when he went on another trip, I'd have to answer no. I understand that isn't the case with many spouses who have been betrayed. For me, I was able to trust Christ to deal with Gene. It was just such an unusual feeling, but I was released from the pressure to have to change him. If he chose to sin and go back to that life, that would be his choice. In that case, I suppose I believed I would have the freedom to move on. But I knew it wasn't my job to change Gene, to make him who I wanted him to be. It was God's job to make Gene into the man He wanted him to be. There was so much freedom in that for me. I didn't think Gene could perform for Christ, but I did believe Christ could work in and through Gene, through us. The Christian life is letting Christ live His life in you and through you. You cannot live the Christian life on your own.

*God did not create marriage to correct our image problems. It is not the responsibility of one spouse to fix or correct the image or the behavior of the other.*

My behavior was not Eldeen's responsibility; nor was it her job to restore my broken image of myself. God didn't create us to need others to validate who we are. Adam wasn't running around the Garden of Eden whining, "I don't know who I am! Give me a woman to tell me." He was connected with the perfect source of his image. The same was true of Eve. And the same is true of you and me. We were all made in God's image, and He longs to show us how He sees us as lovable, individual human beings.

God did not create marriage to correct our image problems. It is not the responsibility of one spouse to fix or correct the image or the behavior of the other.

So often when I am counseling a couple with marital problems, I inevitably hear something like: "If only my husband would do *such-and-such*, I would be secure in who I am." "If only my wife would *blah-blah-blah*, I would be okay."

In other words, both are saying, "If only my spouse would change, I would see myself differently."

So we look to others to prove ourselves acceptable, to help us with the way we see ourselves. Husbands and wives have something to learn. We cannot rely on our partner to fix what we are lacking. We cannot look to our job or children either. No human being, no career, absolutely nothing can meet this inherent need of man and woman but the Lord. Marriage, or any relationship for that matter, does not solve image problems … it reveals them.

After I became a Christian, Eldeen didn't put up with my wisecracks anymore. She called me out when my behavior was inappropriate or hurtful. We had trust issues and forgiveness to work through. Transformation is a process.

All of us will bump into these growing pains—in ourselves and others—no matter how long we walk with the Lord. It is a fact of being human. Remember, the work God is doing in our lives takes a lifetime. God will continue to reveal those parts of ourselves that do not come in line with the image of how He made us. That's a comforting promise for each one of us. We can trust that He "who began a good work in you will carry it on to completion until the day of Christ Jesus" (Philippians 1:6).

## Made in God's Image, Not Each Other's

Our self-image is not the only image that got messed up when the Fall happened. For some reason, we tend to think others should look like us. Let me explain.

In premarital counseling, my goal is to help the engaged couple separate fantasy from reality. I ask each, "What is the image you have of the kind of man/woman you want?" It is a fact that each of us has a picture in our mind of the kind of person we want to marry. But if someone is hoping their fiancé will one day become the image they want, they will only be let down.

Just as harmful is one person trying to live up to the image the other holds for them. Should they marry before dealing with this issue, each will be sorely disappointed. It is just a matter of time before one of them will not be able to live up to this phantom image. Then the conflict begins. That's usually when they come to see me.

Just as there are stages in life, there are stages in a relationship. During the romantic stage, all is rosy. Each person is lost in the excitement of the other. This is the time of attraction and discovery—of the good and the not so good. No matter how hard they may try to hide them, each begins to learn of the other's imperfections. Typically, these shortcomings are excused, overlooked, or dismissed. Little, if anything, is done to resolve differences. As the saying goes, "Love is blind."

Then comes the commitment stage when a relationship moves to a deeper level. Now, all of a sudden, the deficits and imperfections in each other are clearly in focus. They are blatant, glaring, and unmistakable.

In *The Mystery of Marriage*, Mike Mason says this:

> ... love convinces a couple that they are the greatest romance that has ever been, that no two people have ever loved as they do, and that they will sacrifice absolutely anything in order to be together. And then marriage asks them to prove

it. Marriage is the down-to-earth dimension of romance, the translation of a romantic blueprint into costly reality ...

In relationships, commitment is a safety net. This is true of any relationship—in families, friendships, dating, engagements, and marriage. In the safety of commitment, each person opens up more and says what they really think and feel. While these revelations may be freeing for one, they could be disconcerting for the other, resulting in tension. The deeper the commitment, the more intense the tension.

At the point of strain, many couples begin fighting due to unmet expectations and unrealized plans. It isn't long before a power struggle is underway. Where did this wonderful, loving relationship go wrong? It began when they bumped into each other's "imperfectness" and tried to change each other into the image of what they wanted their partner to be.

And this is where we need to stop and remind ourselves of God's perfect plan: Man and woman were created in the image of God, not in the image of each other.

## Root of Inadequacy and Insecurity

Throughout my years of counseling, I've seen an eye-opening pattern in men and women. Multiple times I have heard a wife say, "When my husband does this [whatever the deed may be], it really makes me feel insecure." The husbands come to me with a different complaint. "If only my wife would support me and be behind me all the time, always build me up, then I would feel like an adequate person." Typically, the deep needs I see in men stem from feelings of *inadequacy*. For women, their needs seem to spring from feelings of *insecurity*. There's a reason for this.

As a result of their disobedience, God had different things to say to Adam and to Eve. He informed Eve of the pain of childbirth and that her husband would rule over her. Then He told Adam he would have to work hard, something he'd never had to deal with before (see Genesis 3:16–19).

In the beginning, Adam had dominion over creation (Genesis 1:28). Everything cooperated with him. It was as if his wish was their command. After the Fall, the situation did a 180 degree turnaround. Now Adam had to work to get the land and the creatures to do what he wanted. Nothing cooperated … including woman. This made him feel inadequate.

For the woman, childbirth became painful. Where the man would labor in the fields, the woman would labor in the delivery room. One more thing changed. The woman would now have to submit to her husband, an imperfect man. This made her feel insecure.

What happens when imperfect man is in a relationship with imperfect woman? There is enough fodder for a spectacular fireworks display. When a woman is faced with a man's imperfections, she feels insecure. She then tries to fix his inadequacies to feel secure. When a man is faced with a woman's insecurities, especially when coated with tears, he feels helpless and inadequate. No man wants to be reminded of his inadequacies. No woman wants to feel insecure. It does not take much before this tension sparks a power struggle. The battle is on.

Many of us go through life either trying to disprove our image (I did not want to be seen as an adulterer) or live up to an image that is not true of us. We don't want to look inside to see the real us; there's too much to unpack. But like my pastor and mentor, Stuart Briscoe, used to say, "A life unpacked is not worth living."

I tried to work with a dad several years ago who took himself out of the battle by moving away from his wife and children. There was no hint that he would do anything like this. He had always done everything he was asked, never said "no" to anybody. This man had a sensitive spirit and always tried hard to be what everyone wanted him to be. Then the inevitable occurred; he burned out. When he and I talked, he explained, "I don't know who I am and I don't know what I want." He felt inadequate as a husband and dad, and without a self-image rooted in God's acceptance, he bailed. His wife was left behind to deal with her insecurities on her own.

The root cause of problems in our relationships has little to do with how we see ourselves or the experiences we have had—it is all within ourselves. It all boils down to opening ourselves to examination and allowing God to meet our needs (our inadequacies and insecurities) His way. He must be the One to define our image. Then we have the proper foundation in our relationships for true intimacy to flourish.

Eldeen and I were married in 1963. (Of course, we were just youngsters at the time!) Still, I can honestly tell you I feel like I haven't even begun to understand her true image as a woman. And I am still discovering what my true image is as a man. Eldeen and I will continue to explore and discover and experience each other. That is the great journey of marriage. And the incredible joy!

# Part Two

The Influence of Our Past on
Our Ability to Connect

## CHAPTER 5

# Trauma of Transparency

T RAUMA IS a word commonly used throughout therapy circles. Recently I took twenty-five hours of trauma training from two experts on trauma. And when you get right down to it … who hasn't had trauma one way or another? That goes back to the Fall. We're all born into a broken world. A broken world where perfect doesn't happen. A broken world where trauma, tragedy, and struggles prevail. A broken world with pain in relationships where it doesn't belong. Your marriage is designed to be the safest human relationship possible. But that isn't always the case. If your marriage relationship is disconnected, opening yourself in transparency can be terrifying. I call that the trauma of transparency.

To open ourselves in vulnerability with anyone is scary. We don't know how the other person will respond. Will we be safe in our vulnerability or will we be putting ourselves in harm's way? If you confess your innermost thoughts with your spouse, will he or she react in anger or kindness? Will they understand? Forgive? It is natural that each of us has a certain fear of intimacy.

Added fear of transparency happens when we have something to hide. If we're concerned our confessions will not be received by a safe listening ear, fear prevents us from confessing our hidden secrets. That's understandable. I have learned, however, that we can be hiding things we didn't even know were there. There's a story behind everything, and most of those stories begin early in life. Our self-image and expectations, views of the opposite sex and relationships, are formed in childhood. Much of our difficulty at achieving intimacy in our marriages stems back to patterns and behaviors we experienced as children, mainly from our parents. Such was the case with Savannah. When she came to see me in my office, she was suffering from the trauma of transparency, afraid of letting a man get too close. As we explored her past, we started to discover why.

While most people start dating in high school, the very thought struck fear in Savannah. She did not trust boys romantically. They could be her friends, but nothing else. Over the years, she had had many guy friends. Imagine her distress when she was attracted to one. She wanted him; she feared him. The fear would win, and Savannah would beat a safe retreat. In other words, as a means to protect herself, Savannah would isolate herself, sometimes physically and always emotionally.

"I remember thinking that if someone saw the real me, they could not possibly love me. When it comes to relationships with men, I feel like damaged goods. Undesirable, ugly, useless, revolting—like rotten fruit. You can't wait to throw it away. Fruit is bruised on the outside; I am bruised on the inside. I am afraid of being bruised and damaged more. I don't want to be rejected and thrown away."

If you met Savannah, you would never guess she wrote the above statement. In her late thirties, she is intelligent, talented, and funny, the kind of person who is the life of the party. And she is still single.

Savannah's desire is to be married and have a family. As time goes on, her hope is fading. "I feel like life is simpler without the longing. I know … pain is a part of life … but this pain runs so deep, to want a man, to want a true, intimate relationship, yet have so much fear at the thought of it all. I don't get it." On one hand, Savannah wants an intimate relationship. On the other hand, even the thought of it brings fear. "I don't understand. What is down deep inside me to make me think this way?"

As part of her therapy, Savannah and I looked at her childhood. We started to see an explanation for Savannah's bruised self-image.

Until the day Savannah's father died, Savannah was always a little afraid of him. Her father had virtually no relationship with his children when they were young. He didn't know what to do with kids, so he did nothing at all. An emotional loner, he thought he probably should have never married.

Since their father worked long hours, about the only time the children saw him was on the weekends, and even then the family felt they had to walk on eggshells around him. Although he was never physically violent or emotionally abusive, the children knew they had to stay out of their father's way. He was virtually unavailable and emotionally distant. Although Savannah's father was highly intelligent and successful in his profession, he suffered from depression. The family became used to his black moods, which were tremendously confusing and disruptive. During one episode that lasted three weeks, their father did not look at them or speak to them, as if they were not even there. Each family member racked their brains to figure out what they might have done to make him mad. It usually was something so silly that had set him off. The one that sparked the three weeks of depression? There were no cans of his favorite soda in the fridge.

Still, as is natural for a daughter, Savannah wanted her father's love. But no matter how hard she tried, she never felt like she met his expectations. After getting straight A's on a report card in high school, she waited for her father to sit in his favorite chair after work and notice the report cards on the end table. He looked them over and never said a thing. He went right back to reading the paper, leaving Savannah crushed. Even being perfect didn't seem to be enough to get his attention and his love.

Together, Savannah and I worked through the wounds caused by her father's behavior. Gradually she began to see herself through God's eyes, and her self-image continues to be restored. Just recently, Savannah wanted to take the next step in the healing process. She knew she needed to take a risk emotionally. One friend in particular had caught her interest. She gathered her courage and told him that she had developed strong feelings for him. While he did not return her feelings, Savannah had overcome her fear.

As Savannah waits for the right man, she is actively trusting in the Lord to guide her steps. She acknowledges that the path God has for her may not include a husband, but whatever her marital status, Savannah knows she will continue to take risks. She will no longer believe the lies she understood as a young girl. Savannah no longer sees herself as damaged goods easily dismissed by a distant father. She now knows she is deeply loved and accepted by her Heavenly Father.

As Eldeen and I continue to grow in intimacy, we have recognized, like with Savannah, how much the trauma of our pasts affected our inability to connect intimately in our marriage. Our stories have many similarities with others I've heard from countless clients over the years. Much of the inability for us to be intimate as adults stems back to the conditioning we have experienced as children. I'll let Eldeen share her story first. I expect some of you will relate.

> *Much of the inability for us to be intimate as adults stems back to the conditioning we have experienced as children.*

### Eldeen

I've always equated love as peace, kindness, and gentleness. My motto was: "Think of the other person first, myself second." I was extremely loyal, almost to a fault. Starting with the small things, I was always covering up someone else's mistakes. I have learned this is very common in alcoholic families.

My parents loved me, and I never doubted it. But they were not always there for me. My father was a hard worker and had two jobs. To unwind, he always stopped at the local pub. It was a lot like the television show, "Cheers," where you would go to the bar to meet your buddies.

Eventually my mother joined him there. She could not get him to come home, so the next best thing in her mind was to be with him. Even though we were too young and ill-equipped to do so, my brother and I were left to care for ourselves.

When I hit my teen years, my parents were hitting the height of their alcohol abuse. At the same time, their fighting increased tremendously. Whenever my mother drank she got angry, especially with my father. On the other hand, my father was a happy-go-lucky drunk. Except the few times when my mother flew into a rage and cornered my father. In a defensive manner, he would become physically abusive with her. When that happened I would run to my room and put a pillow over my head. I thought if I wished hard enough, it would all go away.

Though no one told me, I felt it was my responsibility to keep the peace between my parents. I was the peacemaker. My job was to keep them together. I tried to resolve their fights: "Oh Mom, don't you hear what Dad is saying? Dad, don't you see that Mom really means … ?" More than anything, I wanted them to stay married. In actuality, I was parenting my parents when they acted like children.

When I was in high school, I met Gene. I was very attracted to him and appreciated his outgoing nature. I had feelings for him that I never had with anyone else. But looking back, I think we were drawn to each other because of our families' strengths and weaknesses.

Gene grew up very poor and I felt sorry for him. This was a normal response for me because I was used to taking care of people who had problems. I naturally fell into the role of helping him. In return, Gene gave me attention and appreciation. Our relationship seemed like a perfect match. I saw Gene as the high school hero, and I was there to support him. What I did not understand then was that I transferred supporting my parents to supporting Gene, my new love.

Growing up in a chaotic household, it was important to me that my marriage created the perfect family. I wanted safety, security, and calm in the midst of the stresses of life. I wanted a haven. When I met Gene's family, I thought they were the family I had always wanted. As we sat down to dinner with everyone together, there was no fighting or anger. And to top it off, they went to church as a family. I thought I'd found the perfect man from the perfect family. Almost.

Even before we were married, I was well aware of Gene's anger. His outbursts were usually at academics or sports when he was frustrated with his performance. Sometimes he got angry at inanimate things like the car when it broke down, etc. After we got married though, his anger was directed at me. He did not seem to be as thoughtful anymore either. And his drinking was more than I ever realized.

I was direct with Gene when it came to things in our relationship. I am sure he thought at the time that I was trying to make him feel guilty. Three years into our marriage, I wondered how our marriage could make it in the stress of the world. I grew up in a dysfunctional family and I wanted to make a functional family in my marriage. That is when I came to the Lord.

Eldeen was right. I was an angry person, afraid of being known—really known. Unwilling to look at myself honestly, I covered up my feelings of inadequacy with my anger. Take that, my competitive nature, and a football field, then watch out! I was an angry man on the field with almost no regard for my body. With the same kind of abandon, I threw myself into work, hungry to be the best. Unfortunately, as I was succeeding in work, I was failing in my marriage, adding to my wife's feelings of insecurity.

Also, Eldeen's first impressions of my family weren't accurate. I didn't have the perfect family. Far from it. I guess you could say I come from a long line of needy men. My father grew up in a household with a mother who ruled the roost. It was not uncommon for my grandmother to put down and demean my grandfather, even in front of their children. I am sure this treatment left him feeling "less of a man." Typically, when men feel inadequate, they are driven by a hunter instinct. Men want to get women to give themselves (while men fear giving themselves to women). As a result of growing up in this environment, both my father and his brother established their masculinity by conquering women.

Shortly after my father met my mother, he got her pregnant. He was reluctant to marry her, but my uncle talked him into it. From the very beginning, my mother was insecure in their relationship, not really feeling loved or wanted. Within a few years, a young family was formed with three boys (I was the middle child). It did not take long before tragedy struck, when my younger brother, only eighteen months old, drowned. My grandmother blamed my mother. "If you had been watching him, this never would have happened." Never mind that my father was in a bar at the time.

By this time, my father's parents talked them into moving onto their farm. It was extremely hard for my mother to live with her in-laws. If she wanted to buy anything, she had to go to my grandmother for the money. Then my sister was born. As a newborn, she developed a high fever that left her deaf and cognitively delayed. My mother was distraught. She worried constantly that something else might befall them at any moment. Fear was now her constant companion.

Growing up, church was part of our life, but it didn't seem to have a positive influence on my parents. My mother was always helping others out and then complaining about it. She would put herself in positions to be taken advantage of and used. She did not seem to have any boundaries or self-respect. For my mother, love was doing, not affection or hugging. She had a way of manipulating others to get her needs met. She would not just come out and ask for something; she used guilt. So often I felt trapped by it. In her later years, she'd call and instead of saying, "I miss you, can you come visit me?" she'd say, "Forget where I live?" As they always did, these statements made me feel guilty, then angry. So I would give in and do what she wanted, feeling manipulated the whole time. This exchange was very typical of our lifelong communication.

My dad would go out witnessing and talk about Christ— without knowing Him. There was a weakness in my dad's life that he never dealt with, a weakness that controlled and crippled him emotionally. If we think of life as a race, my father ran and did not accomplish anything. In reality, he was a prisoner to his own pain and hurt from his past. He didn't understand the grace of God until the very end of his life. In terms of a career, my dad never succeeded at anything he did. His mother had a way of sabotaging him and his efforts. Consequently, we didn't have much when my parents moved off the farm. We were poor. In fact, there were times when we did not have any electricity to heat the house in the winter (something vital in Milwaukee). Sometimes, we did not have enough food.

I don't remember any intimacy in my parents' relationship. In fact, my brother and I never knew the date of their wedding anniversary; there was never any celebration. During their entire marriage, my father was never faithful to my mother. However, I didn't know that until I was off at college and my father left home, never to return.

Over the years, although I sent my father money, he wouldn't come to visit us. So a few times, I took my children across the country to visit him. With these visits, among other things, I wanted our children to see me make steps toward a father who deserted me. This is an important part of the healing process. I especially want Robbie to remember my example when he deals with aspects of his abandonment by his birth parents (we adopted him when he was just fourteen months old). Sadly, my father was living in the past. All he could talk about was my brother's and my accomplishments in high school athletics.

It took me a while to recognize and overcome the legacy my father left me. My father was a soft, considerate, kind person. But he never knew who he really was. Neither did I. I come from a family of adulterers. Like my father and others who came before me, a part of me was trying to prove I was a man by conquering women. I did not have an understanding of what it meant for a man to hang in and persevere. The Bible is very clear that sin can be passed from one generation to the next. Before I knew it, as a young man I was already following in my father's footsteps. And it took me a long time to process the pain and hurt he caused me, until I was finally able to forgive my father.

Two weeks before my father died, he and I talked on the phone. Through his tears, he asked me to forgive him. I said, "I've already forgiven you. That's not the issue." I went on to share the gospel with him. Then my brother had the opportunity to pray with our dad and give him assurance of his salvation.

I wrote the following poem about my father after his death.

## Once Knew a Man

*Once knew a man*
*who was strong*
*who worked the earth on his German parents' farm.*
*Once knew a man*
*who had a big, warm smile*
*who was easygoing and affectionate.*

*Once knew a man*
*who went to church and read*
*his Bible, who even went on*
*church visitations.*
*Once knew a man*
*Who worried a lot*
*Who would never fight*
*Who tried to keep the peace when the neighbors fought.*
*Once knew a man*
*Who when his future daughter-in-law met him,*
*Thought: I hope my sons will be like him.*
*Once knew a man*
*Who would drop all*
*That he was doing to help others.*
*Once knew a man*
*Who would feel so bad that he could not provide*
*Who would leave church out of shame and guilt*
*Once knew a man*
*Who became more cynical and more bitter*
*When his efforts went unnoticed.*
*Once knew a man*
*who started blaming*
*Others for his lack of success.*
*Once knew a man*
*Who started not to come home sometimes*
*Then, just left.*
*I didn't see the man I once knew much after that.*

*A few times.*
*When I saw him, the man I once knew was old and fragile.*
*He never succeeded. He was poor.*
*All he talked about was the past.*
*Never talked about why he left.*
*Never talked about who he was.*
*Then I got a call*
*The man I once knew was dying.*
*When I called him, he was crying.*
*Said he was sorry.*
*Sorry he messed up my life.*
*Sorry he ran away.*
*"Will you forgive me?" he asked.*
*As the time ticked away, I stopped.*
*I said to this man I once knew,*
*"I did, a long time ago."*
*Will you accept God's forgiveness?*
*Will you accept Christ?*
*This man I once knew had betrayed his wife.*
*This man I once knew abandoned his children.*
*This man I once knew deserted his disabled daughter.*
*This man I once knew was my dad.*
*My heart shouts, Why?*
*Who were you afraid of?*
*Of your wife or your children or yourself?*
*Why did you wait until your death bed*
*To deal with your fear?*

*Please do not be sorry for me.*
*Maybe, we should feel sorry for the man I once knew.*
*Maybe, at times, I would like to feel sorry for myself.*
*For the man I once knew brought a penetrating*
*Pain and deep loss to my life.*
*For my dad was just that, the man I once knew.*
*Yet through this deep hurt and loss,*
*God came.*
*So, now I know a Dad, a Father*
*Who will never leave me or forsake me.*

I do not have the appropriate words to express my gratitude to God for intervening as Heavenly Father in my life. If it were not for the grace of God, I would have destroyed my marriage.

How did my childhood home condition me in the area of intimacy? How did Eldeen's? We couldn't be transparent with each other because we'd both buried fears and believed lies about ourselves. We took on roles that we were never meant to carry. Eldeen became the caregiver, the peacemaker, prone to independence. I became the guilty conqueror, convinced I needed to build myself up in my own strength. And as a result of my mother's manipulation, to this day it is difficult for me to say "No" to someone. I can see how easy it is for me to be manipulated. I can stop it, but it is still hard. The pull to please is a strong one. For both me and Eldeen—and perhaps for you as well—the idea of being transparent, of opening up and sharing our deepest thoughts and feelings, felt too traumatic for each of us.

Thankfully, God has helped me to face my inadequacies honestly and has given me the strength to repent and heal from the damage caused during my childhood. The same thing happened for Eldeen. It's only because of our personal relationships with God and experiencing His healing that Eldeen and I can now connect in open transparency, safe and free to be ourselves in our marriage relationship.

As a counselor, I have worked with hundreds of people whose lives were shaped by betrayal, abandonment, and desertion. I can relate to their pain. I understand the distorted images they have of themselves. I offer them hope and help them make changes to be all they were created to be. I can do this because I found the same hope and change in Jesus Christ. He wants to do the same for you.

God has a path for you to walk. It is as unique as you are. But each of God's children will share this aspect to their journeys—facing the fear of intimacy.

In His love, God allows us to make a choice. We will all come to a crossroad in our lives, and it will reveal two paths to walk down—one the old way, one the new. The old way is to keep protecting ourselves—to hang on to the fear and mechanisms we have developed in the flesh. It might be anger and bitterness, isolation, or constantly looking for another human relationship that will satisfy us. Because this way is familiar, it may appear deceptively safer.

The new way is to give up our control mechanisms to God and let Him teach us the way of true intimacy. For all of us, this is an unknown road, uncharted territory. We walk it by faith, not by sight.

How were you conditioned during your childhood? Do you see any similar patterns in what we've shared? In the chapters ahead, we will examine many more factors that threaten or damage marital intimacy.

So far we've looked at the common desire we all have for intimacy in our marriages. We've acknowledged that pain in marriage relationships and the fear of intimacy are inevitable because of the Fall of mankind in the Garden of Eden. We understand how God made us in His image and that we can experience true intimacy with Him and our marriage partner, but that obstacles prevent that. Next we're going to explore those obstacles in more detail.

CHAPTER 6

# Pain and Protection

T HE NATURAL human response to pain is avoidance. If
something hurts, we want it to stop. And fast. If at all
possible, we will try to avoid what caused the pain. It only
takes a child one time to learn not to touch a hot stove. We
have the same response to emotional pain. When our feelings
have been hurt, we do everything we can to stop the pain
and to avoid that situation in the future.

Children come into this world totally helpless. They need
food, shelter, security, care, and love. Parents are to provide
these necessities. As children grow, so does their world. It is
the parents' job to provide guidance for the children's safety.
When a child is appropriately disciplined, he or she learns
the art of discernment and self-control. Children learn to
avoid bigger dangers in the future by experiencing pain from
smaller dangers in childhood.

Parents use pain—both physical and emotional—to teach
their children right from wrong. Appropriate to age and

temperament, punishment can range from a spanking (physical pain) to a loss of privileges such as time-out, restriction, and grounding (emotional pain). If you obey, there is no pain, and you keep doing what is right. If you disobey … well, hopefully it will only take one time (we parents know that is not always the case). You can say we are shaped by pain. It has its positive side.

Then there is the negative side of pain. In childhood, many of us have experienced some type of pain far greater and deeper than any punishment for disobedience, and that pain has carried into our marriage relationships.

When it comes to experiencing negative pain, there is a marked difference between how adults and children deal with it. Children do not have control over their circumstances. Without proper guidance, they do not have the ability to put painful circumstances in perspective. Negative pain can cause confusion from early on. For children to thrive, they need a home environment that is stable and loving, where they feel protected and safe.

*The natural human response to pain is avoidance. If something hurts, we want it to stop. And fast. If at all possible, we will try to avoid what caused the pain.*

Children instinctively know when their home is unstable. As a result, they suffer emotional pain. We have all heard the statistics that one out of two marriages will end in divorce. That's the first marriage. Second and third marriages tend to fail at even a higher rate.[9] But long before a divorce makes this estimation a reality, there is a breakdown in the marriage relationship, possibly going back for many years. It is no secret that many of these poor, unhappy, marital relationships never end in divorce. They are husband and wife in name only. Just two people sharing no intimacy living under the same roof. So many unmet expectations. So much disappointment. So much hurt, especially to the children growing up in troubled homes.

Recently, I was counseling a family in which there was a tremendous amount of discord between the mother and father. There was anger, outbursts, and threats of divorce. Contrary to what many parents think, from a very young age, children know when there is a problem between Mom and Dad. In this family, one of their children developed a habit which bordered on obsessive-compulsive disorder. Every morning before school, their daughter required they write out their personal schedules for the day. She'd then fold the papers and shove them in the outer pocket of her backpack, which she checked between every class period. She was obsessed with knowing where her parents were. Her parents became concerned when they noticed the ritualistic way in which she was behaving.

Concerned that one of her parents might leave, this young girl developed a habit to alleviate her fear. She was unable to deal with the emotional pain, so she was doing the only thing she knew to feel safe. If you grew up in a troubled home that was filled with conflict, you may have developed your own ways of dealing with the negative pain.

As children grow, other adults are called on to provide care when the children are away from their parents—relatives, babysitters, neighborhood adults, clergy, teachers, and coaches, to name a few. We expect all of these caregivers to have the child's best interest in mind and to always be there to protect the child. Sadly, we know that is not always true. We are all keenly aware of the pain—physical and emotional—that innocent children suffer at the hands of abusive adults.

I want to say right here that I am not bashing parents or community leaders. I am just stating facts. All of us are imperfect people living in an imperfect world. All of us will be let down or hurt by someone we love and trust. And every single one of us will cause pain, most of the time unintentionally, to someone we love.

What each of us needs to identify within our own lives is the pain so traumatic it altered our life as a child and the negative effects that are still hanging on well into adulthood. What negative pain can cause a child to mature into an adult who struggles with intimacy? Negative pain can wound a child physically or emotionally or both at the same time.

When a child is physically abused—beaten, tossed around, knocked on the head—what message does this send about his self-worth? A fractured bone or bruised arm caused by a dad who is supposed to be a loving protector sends conflicting, confusing, negative messages to a child. The worst physical abuse violates a child's sexual innocence. (Sexual molestation is such a painful violation on children, it warrants its own chapter. See Chapter 8). Many victims of childhood physical abuse establish an overprotective wall around themselves when it comes to physical touch. They avoid hugs or sitting too close to others, for example. Physical intimacy can be uncomfortable for grownups who were physically abused as children.

Extreme physical pain leaves lifelong scars, both bodily and emotionally. But there are also childhood wounds that show no physical mark. Many people who struggle with intimacy as an adult were emotionally wounded as children.

Emotional pain can be inflicted in two ways: by a deliberate act or by neglect.

## Deliberate Emotional Pain

Slapping a child is a deliberate action that leaves physical and emotional pain. There are other ways children are deliberately wounded, leaving deep emotional scars no one else can see. Negative emotional pain comes through harsh words, control, manipulation, and violation of privacy, to name a few.

The father of one of my clients exacted control through his angry outbursts; her mother maintained control by her strictness. My client's mother was preoccupied with keeping order in the house, afraid of her husband's anger. If the children misbehaved, they would be punished, as would their mother.

The mother had to control the children in order to escape the backlash from her husband. So my client learned not to confront but to conform, which caused her conflict with intimacy in her adult years. This woman suffered for years as a result of her dad's self-centered anger and her mother's self-protective control. Were these actions deliberate? Yes. The parents inflicted emotional pain through their actions, attitudes, and words. I've seen this scenario played out over and over with my clients.

I've also observed that even abandonment can be deliberate. The following story is one of the saddest displays of emotional pain through abandonment I've ever dealt with.

An afternoon drive for young Brandon and his sister soon turned horrific. Without warning, Brandon's father locked them in the house and did not come back. Can you imagine? The person who was to nurture and protect Brandon and his sister discarded them like some unwanted piece of trash.

To this day, Brandon does not trust anyone. He believes nobody cares about him but himself. In response, Brandon has walled off a part of himself that he will not let anybody touch because he does not want to be hurt like when he was a child.

That childhood desertion taught Brandon that he was not worth anything. The attitude that comes across to other people from Brandon is that they are not worth anything either. But it all stems from the fact that he believes that about himself. He actually reflects to others what he thinks of himself.

Brandon does not believe he is loved and has no clue how to receive love. Other life experiences have only validated his feelings. In relationship after relationship, he keeps repeating the same thing. He will get just so close, then gets out. As soon as conflict arises, he runs away … literally.

Even though his father seriously hurt him, Brandon can move past the pain. It does not have to affect the rest of his life and relationships. The process will take time, but no one has to be a prisoner to his or her pain. That is the hope that God has for each and every one of us, whether the pain inflicted upon us was deliberate or a result of neglect.

## Emotional Pain of Neglect

More often than not, the emotional pain we experience is a result of what others don't do rather than what they do. More people are wounded by the lack of love and protection in their homes than by blatant abuse.

Ryan grew up with a father who never listened. Whenever Ryan tried to talk to him, his father would just walk away. Ryan wanted his father's attention and never got it. Ryan naturally felt his father did not love him.

Recently, Ryan began a conversation with his wife, Maggie. She did not like where the discussion was headed (she hated conflict), so she walked away. As Ryan recalled this incident, it was as if a switch had been flipped. Ryan went ballistic. He followed Maggie outside to continue the fight. In order to keep the argument from their kids, they went into the storage shed behind the house. Before long, they found themselves locked in an embrace. No, it is not quite what you think. They were so angry they had begun wrestling! In my counseling experience, I've learned this is not uncommon. I've had numerous clients describe finding themselves in physical tussles, their anger and desperation turning physical.

Ryan and Maggie did not hurt each other, but suddenly Ryan was struck by a revelation. When Maggie walked away from the argument, Ryan perceived that act as a rejection of him. It tapped into those long-buried hurts from his father's rejection. Ryan couldn't stand it when anyone, especially Maggie, didn't pay attention to him.

Ryan had been depending on his wife to make up for the emotional pain of neglect his father had caused. He was trying to force Maggie to pay attention to him when, in actuality, he was pushing her away emotionally.

The extreme expression of his need for Maggie's attention brought Ryan up short. How could he wrestle his own wife? Ryan says he melted when the Lord reminded him that He was the One who could heal the wounds, not Maggie. This was the breakthrough Ryan needed.

Ryan shifted his dependency from his wife to the Lord. Where he had been looking to Maggie to fix his hurt, he allowed Christ to fix it—the right way. This one change in thinking actually changed the whole dynamic of their intimacy.

What Ryan had been experiencing is common to adults

who were neglected as children. When a parent is unavailable or distant emotionally, the child registers many of the same emotions and develops coping mechanisms as if he or she had been physically deserted.

## Emotional Pain of Abandonment

Desertion or abandonment produce severe forms of emotional pain in children. They simply cannot understand why the person who was supposed to love and protect them didn't follow through.

From the age of five, Tim's childhood had been spent outside the stability of a safe home and loving relationships. This left Tim a tough, scrappy little boy who had to grow up quickly. Tim learned to be resilient, already working to support himself in his early teens.

Many years later in the counseling room, I sat across from a successful businessman who was bankrupt in his relationships. Over the years, Tim had received affirmation from his work, so that is where he gave himself. After many years of marriage, his wife wanted a divorce and Tim did not know why. He thought everything was fine. He was blind to a part of himself that never developed: the ability to connect intimately with another person, much less his wife.

It saddens me to report that Tim's marriage ended in divorce, and they are no longer continuing the counseling process. Still, I pray Tim learns how to experience intimacy. It's never too late.

Another source of emotional pain and feelings of abandonment for children is divorce, especially if one of the parents does not stay involved in the child's life. The emotional pain of divorce is different for the adults and children involved. To children, divorce is a form of desertion.

Recently a divorced mother called me with concern for her twenty-year-old son. He had not seen his biological father since he was a toddler. Now she was seeing problems in his life, which she attributed to the desertion of his father. She was right. Her son could not keep a relationship—either through his own sabotage or moving on when a young woman got too close.

Divorce inflicts emotional pain on the children and takes away their protection; at least that's the way children often see it. Judith Wallerstein, PhD, has been studying the long-term effects of divorce on families. In her book, *Second Chances*, she states:

> Divorce is a different experience for children and adults because the children lose something that is fundamental to their development—the family structure. The family comprises the scaffolding upon which children mount successive development stages, from infancy into adolescence. It supports their psychological, physical, and emotional ascent into maturity. When that structure collapses, the children's world is temporarily without supports. And children, with a

vastly compressed sense of time, do not know that the chaos is temporary. What they do know is that they are dependent on the family. Whatever its shortcomings, children perceive the family as the entity that provides the support and protection that they need. With divorce that structure breaks down, leaving children who feel alone and very frightened about the present and the future.[10]

Children of divorce process the same grief as if one of their parents had died. The parent is still living, though not completely in the child's life anymore. Initially, a grieving child will be in denial, holding out incredible hope that their parents will get back together. Next, they become angry. The final stage in the grief process is acceptance, being resigned to the fact that their parents' marriage is over.

If children continue to deny the reality of the divorce, they will deny their feelings of anger and hurt. At this point they will turn inward, becoming depressed or fearful. Depending on the particular personality bent of the child, different self-protection responses arise. When a child is fearful, they may act out and begin hitting others. They could also become sensitive to ridicule due to being abandoned. Oftentimes, they will be afraid to be themselves for fear of being rejected. Many children of divorce end up trying to please everyone. You can see how these fears and behaviors would affect a person's ability to be intimate as an adult.

Typically, I see these symptoms in adults who grew up in a divorced household:

- **Isolation.** A common response is to pull away from all relationships, keeping others at arm's length, so to speak. Of course, this leads to a very lonely life.
- **Smothering.** The opposite of isolation. The individual becomes overly absorbed in another person, clinging and controlling until the object of their "affection" pulls away.
- **Fear of failure.** Individuals fear getting involved in intimate relationships. Before relationships have a chance to fail, they actually sabotage them.
- **Repeated failures.** The same failures are repeated over and over again, leaving the individual with no idea why.

As you can see, there are many ways in which a child can be deserted or abandoned. There are physical ways, such as through the death of a parent, divorce, or being put up for adoption. And there are emotional ways, through neglect. No matter the form of abandonment, many children grow into adulthood feeling that something is missing in their lives.

When a parent is unavailable or distant emotionally, the child registers many of the same emotions and develops coping mechanisms as if he or she has been physically deserted. If not dealt with, those wounds—and their effect—carry into adulthood.

Kurt came to see me, deeply concerned with a lack of commitment and contentment in his marriage. He confessed his desire for attention from women other than his wife. As we looked at his childhood, we uncovered a wound that had never healed. Kurt had no idea that this childhood pain drove him to seek love from woman after woman.

When Kurt was a young boy, his mother moved out of the house and divorced his father—for another woman. The desertion of his mother to a gay lifestyle had a ripple effect on the family. Kurt's father began going from woman to woman to fix his own pain. This reaction is not uncommon. In order to prove they are still desirable, many rejected individuals will seek the attention and affection of another person. This drive is amplified when a person is left by their spouse for a same-sex partner.

Kurt "lost" his mother when she moved out. He also "lost" his father, who was now busy seeking a relief for his pain. Experiencing a form of abandonment from both parents was a double whammy for Kurt. It is no wonder he began to feel insecure.

During this time, Kurt was developing his identity as a man. Whenever Kurt visited with his mother, she focused her attention on his looks. The only way she knew to show love was to give Kurt things. So it was no surprise Kurt got attention from women through his looks. His body became the means of getting love.

From his teenage years on, Kurt had to have a female in

his life. He was so insecure he did not want to be on his own, even for a second. As a relationship was ending, Kurt would make sure to start another relationship before the current one ended. Overlapping relationships caused Kurt to begin leading a double life. As is often the case, this pattern doesn't necessarily go away once a person gets married.

Kurt believed finding the right woman would end his almost compulsive need for a woman. That special woman would save him from living a life of duplicity. But not long after he was married, Kurt felt he was not getting enough attention and thought he was missing out on something. The temptation was too much for him, and he sought the attention from past girlfriends. He was lying and covering up. His double life continued.

This type of lifestyle creates such confusion over legitimate feelings of love. Oftentimes, when a person has developed a habit of getting attention and love in the wrong way, they will begin to be repulsed by their spouse (the right relationship to experience love). This happened to Kurt.

Over the course of Kurt's counseling sessions, Kurt came to grips with the fact that his lifestyle was a lie. His eyes have been opened to the fact that he suffered emotional abandonment as a teen and adopted false ideas in an attempt to soothe his pain. Fortunately, Kurt is in the process of discovery and change. He is beginning to see himself the way God sees him, and he is letting Him work in his life to heal the emotional pain his parents had caused, as well as the pain he inflicted on himself.

Many wounded people who suffered emotional pain in childhood feel as if they have a giant hole in their heart. How they fill that void is as varied as the individuals themselves. I am here to tell you, trying to fix the hole in the wrong way will not bring you any closer to the love and intimacy you desperately seek.

Some people who have come to see me are on their second and third marriages. They have never dealt with their childhood pain of being deserted by a parent through divorce. As a result, they continue to live out that early desertion in their adult relationships.

You have another choice. Although it may not be easy, working through the emotional pain stemming from your childhood can open beautiful doors of intimacy for you and your spouse.

CHAPTER 7

# Chains of ... Love?

WHILE SOME spouses struggle with intimacy because of being abandoned or physically or emotionally wounded as children, others struggle because they've been given too much attention in a harmful way. The opposite of abandonment is smothering, or emotional enmeshment. I see this most often between mothers and sons, fathers and daughters. Either way, enmeshment creates a painful dilemma for the child, especially as the child matures into adulthood and gets married.

## Emotional Enmeshment with a Parent

Emotional enmeshment happens when a parent depends on a child for emotional support. If a parent allows or sets up a child to meet their emotional needs, that parent is committing emotional incest. And the child's understanding of self as well as the ability to have an intimate marriage as an adult are damaged as a result. A parent's support for emotional pain should be met by their spouse or another adult, not a child. I cannot stress this enough. Parents need to go to God, other adults, or professionals, not their own children, for help.

At times I have counseled individuals who have just gone through a divorce, and there is one piece of parenting advice I strongly stress: Do not share your hurts and pains of the divorce with your children. Don't seek comfort from them either.

I know this is easy to say and harder to do. Especially if the child is very empathetic. Many mothers have told me their child has said to them, "I will protect you, Mommy. I will take care of you." Of course, these words would speak comfort to a wounded mother. The same sentiment would be comforting to a dad if his child tried to soothe Dad's pain. But it is at that point when the parent needs to respond to their child in this way: "I appreciate that you are concerned for me, but we need to go to God with that need. God will protect me and take care of my needs. You are my child; you are not responsible to fix my emotional pain."

This might strike a chord with you. A parent leaning too heavily on a child for support happens frequently. Emotional enmeshment can be disastrous. Many of my clients have had to learn how to separate from an enmeshed parent before they could pursue an intimate partnership with their spouse.

After waiting several decades, Hunter got married for the first time. It was a wonderful beginning for Hunter and his new bride, Teresa. They were so relieved that the wedding went off without a hitch ... because it almost didn't.

During their pre-marital counseling, it surfaced that Hunter's mother was overly emotionally dependent on him, especially as he was her only son. But it was not until we were into the depths of the counseling process that Hunter realized the extent of his bondage to his mother. Finally, he was able to see how he had blocked himself off from intimacy as a result.

During their engagement, Hunter continued to let Teresa more and more into his heart. As I explained that his priority of loyalty would be to Teresa alone, Hunter began to set healthy boundaries with his mother. She had never liked Teresa (I am sure she would not like any woman who might "take away" her son), but as the wedding neared, she went into an emotional tirade.

A week before the ceremony, Hunter's mother tried to sabotage it. She did all kinds of things to make him feel guilty for neglecting her, even going so far as telling him she'd seen Teresa with another man.

Manipulation is a common tactic used by the needy parent to try to maintain control. One man told me his mother actually faked a heart attack when she learned he was going to get married. He got married anyway and has been married now for many years.

To help them in their new life together, Hunter and Teresa are continuing the counseling process. They know that they will continue to reap the consequences of relationships in their families of origin. Hunter will need to persist in setting boundaries with his mother. This will be crucial if and when they have children.

It is important to note that I am not talking about a close relationship between parent and child. It is normal to enjoy being with our children and to love them, at all ages. We feel good when they express their love and appreciation to us. As the parent, it is our job to nurture, guide, teach, love, and provide for our children as they grow—and then release them to live their own adult lives.

With emotional incest, a parent becomes overly enmeshed with their child. The line between adult and child becomes blurred. The child is put in a position to satisfy the needs of their parent—needs children are not equipped or created by God to meet. When a parent leans on a child for emotional support, the needs of the child are ignored and neglected. As they grow, these substitute "spouses" are trapped, finding it difficult to betray their parent to bond with another. They also haven't learned how to deal with their own emotional needs.

Andrew loves the Lord and has an extensive knowledge of the Bible. But he has never been able to bring himself to commit to a woman. Andrew is a victim of emotional incest. When he was growing up, Andrew's mother relied on him to meet her emotional needs. To this day, she is still inappropriately dependent on him.

Early on, Andrew felt trapped by his emotions. It was like bondage to him to always be there for his mother. As a result, Andrew developed a tremendous apprehension or fear of being in bondage to another woman. He will not put himself in a position to bond on a deep, emotional level.

I can see the effect of Andrew's emotional bondage, but he does not. He still lives in denial. Andrew may never face reality, which would leave him perpetually single and isolated. If he decides he wants to have a relationship with a woman, he will come to a crisis point. It is then that he must make a choice. If he faces the truth, he may be able to break through and experience a bonding, rather than bondage.

For both men and women, the result of emotional incest is bondage. When it comes to relationships with men, a woman will find herself replaying the role she had in childhood. She is left unable to relate to a man on an adult, intimate level. Most likely she will fear not being in control, but she must let go of her control to trust God and a man to be there for her. She will have to come to the point of redefining what it means to be a wife instead of an emotional caretaker.

For a man, emotional incest leaves him in the precarious position of fearing intimacy and not knowing how to let a woman into his life emotionally. He has been the responsible one in an enmeshed relationship, carrying a weight of care for his parent that isn't his to carry. The unhealthy burden causes a man to wall off his heart because he doesn't feel he can carry any more. In addition, he doesn't feel the freedom to share his own heart. His mother needed him to be there for her, not the other way around. When a man can't seem to allow himself to be intimate with a woman on an emotional level, enmeshment with a parent is often the root problem.

Emotional incest leaves a person with confused boundaries of responsibility. For the adult who has grown up with an overly enmeshed parent, he or she must begin to understand what is and is not their responsibility when it comes to meeting someone's needs. They must be particularly careful not to let someone use them.

## Caretaker of Feelings

A flag is raised in my mind when I hear this statement from a client: "I never wanted to hurt my dad's (or mom's) feelings." There is a strong possibility that when these clients were children they could never be honest with their parents because they felt they had to "caretake" their parent's feelings. The clients could not be themselves; they could not be children. Their responsibility to care for a parent was too great.

As a little girl, Valerie found herself thrust into the role of surrogate mother of her younger sister when her drug-addicted mother suddenly abandoned the family.

In an instant, Valerie went from child to "mother," since her father needed her to care for her sister. In addition, her father began sharing his thoughts and feelings with Valerie about what he was going through. The daughter became the father's emotional confidant.

Valerie's father was getting his emotional needs met through Valerie, needs that should have been met by a wife. Obviously, Valerie felt special because of his attention and need of her. While this emotionally incestuous situation increased her level of maturity, Valerie lost her childhood. As a teenager, Valerie rebelled against her father's authority and got involved in drinking, drugs, and sex.

As Valerie began dating, she had a distant, aloof, take-charge attitude. She gave the impression of "running the ship" and being in control. It is no mistake that she attracted and married a reserved, quiet, introverted man. He did not force himself on her or demand much at all. Due to her strengths, she married a needy man. For many years, this arrangement felt good to Valerie because she retained the control.

At the same time, Valerie began to realize that she and her husband had intimacy issues, but she had no idea why. Her husband felt he was not able to be himself with her. Valerie had no idea what it meant to be vulnerable and to depend on a man. Her independence actually caused her husband to feel he was not needed. So he began to escape into his own world through drinking.

I have helped Valerie understand how her relationship with her father affected her and kept her distanced emotionally from her husband. As hard as it is for her, she continues to work on allowing her husband to be responsible. She is beginning to back off from controlling, permitting herself to be dependent on him.

Caretaker women, it seems, frequently have trouble in their marriages. These relationships have no intimacy because it is not a relationship of wife /husband but of parent/child. Women will play the role of parent with their husbands to fix them and make them what they think they should be. At the same time, men who need to see themselves as the hero fall into this same trap. In their "caretaking," they actually exercise control, operating more as parent than husband. Inevitably, in either case, a power struggle will ensue, threatening the marriage.

You will find many caretaker children who get into caretaker professions as adults: missionaries, nurses, etc. It is when you look at their family system growing up that you see this dysfunction. Someone put them in a position of being responsible to care for others. Of course, this is not true of everyone in a caretaker profession, but you would be surprised just how many have come from this type of dysfunctional family.

## Leave and Cleave

With a desire to be helpful, Caleb gave himself to others in serving the Lord. But Caleb was unable to give himself to his wife, Allison. He could not be emotionally intimate because he was afraid to be himself with her. This fear of intimacy with his wife made him vulnerable to giving himself to another.

It all began innocently enough over the internet. Before long, Caleb and his online friend began sending each other email. They shared confidences and became emotionally involved. Whether consummated or not, an affair is still an affair. And it was threatening his marriage.

As Caleb explained in the counseling room, he felt he could never please Allison. He would make an effort to get close to her and then abruptly pull away. For years, he lived with the tension of wanting to be intimate with his wife and then feeling inadequate to satisfy her emotionally.

I asked Caleb to describe his relationship with his mother. His answer gave telling insight into his current problem with Allison. At some point in his parent's marriage, his father had been unfaithful. They did not get a divorce, but their relationship had died.

Caleb then became his mother's confidant. Except for anything sexual, Caleb's mother shared everything in her life with him. His mother put him in a position of being responsible for something God never intended him to handle. Caleb could not become his mother's husband emotionally. If he could not be in that role for his mother, is it any wonder he felt that he wouldn't be able to be there for his wife?

In order to understand Caleb's situation, we must go back to what God said to Adam after He had created Eve and presented her to her new husband. "That is why a man leaves his father and mother and is united to his wife; and they become one flesh" (Genesis 2:24). With those words, God's plan for marriage was established. First, a man must leave his parents. He is no longer under their authority. Next, he must cleave to his wife. We do not use the word "cleave" in our everyday language, but it means to cling or adhere to, *to be faithful.* The "leaving and cleaving" process is a transference of loyalty from the family of origin to the new family-to-be.

In Caleb's case, he did not leave and cleave. He was still emotionally attached to his mother. Caleb was smack dab in the middle of a loyalty triangle, trying to be faithful to both his mother and his wife. But as you know, when you try to please two people, you end up pleasing neither. Because he had not "left" his mother, there was no way Caleb could fully cleave (or be faithful) to Allison. We need no other evidence of this than his online affair.

For marriages to start out on the right foot, this loyalty transition must take place. Before our daughter, Deanna, got married, I sat down to talk with her husband-to-be. I told Blair that Eldeen and I were letting our daughter go. "When I give Deanna your hand in the ceremony, her first line of loyalty will be to you, not to us. If you ever feel that we interfere with Deanna's loyalty to you, you have the right to come to us."

I've seen many victims of emotional enmeshment with a parent move beyond the unhealthy dynamics with their offending parent. For many people, recognizing the unhealthy attachment is enough to say "no more." Others have taken longer to work their way out of the entangled parental relationship. And even more spouses have done the hard work of recognizing the beliefs and patterns they developed as a result of being Mom's or Dad's emotional caretaker, and are now experiencing renewed intimacy in their marriage.

CHAPTER 8

# The Ultimate Betrayal

CYNTHIA NEVER felt loved or accepted by her father. She felt she could never measure up to his ideal of perfection. Often, she'd be yelled at if there was even the slightest infraction of "Dad's unknown rules." She'd get in trouble for things she didn't even do. Yet, like any little girl, she still craved and hoped for her father's approval. When Cynthia was a young child, she developed a close relationship with an older man in their church. He treated Cynthia like a grandchild. He let her sit beside him in church and always had a stick of gum for her in his pocket. He invited Cynthia over to his house for tea and cookies, and she innocently thought he represented the love and acceptance she was not getting from inside her family. This man filled the void in Cynthia's life left by her father.

To Cynthia, this man was her friend, but he was also much more. "He was the only father figure who accepted me without any expectations," Cynthia told me in a counseling session. And he and Cynthia shared a secret. He was sexually abusing her. He had her perform certain sexual acts on him while he touched her inappropriately. He told Cynthia not to tell anyone because this was their secret. She did not. In fact, Cynthia never thought anything was wrong with this secret. How could it be wrong when she was finally getting love and attention from a special person? This abuse went on for two years and ended only when Cynthia and her family moved to a new town.

I have counseled many women and men who have come from situations similar to Cynthia's. Childhood sexual abuse is betrayal. It occurs when an individual who has a position of authority in a relationship of trust manipulates a child to get his/her needs met. The victimizer may be a neighbor, teacher, coach, or even worse, a clergyman or, like Cynthia, a member of a church.

When counseling a victim of physical or sexual abuse, the first thing I address is that the abuse was not their fault. Sexual abuse occurs where someone who has authority uses a child to get his or her needs met in the wrong way. The perpetrator is in control, not the child. The child invariably does not see it that way. Children blame themselves for what has happened to them. They believe they must have done something wrong, or that person would not have taken advantage of them. Sexual abuse victims, especially from incest—a family member—live with incredible guilt. For many victims, it takes a lifetime to get over the emotional pain. They are the survivors. Unfortunately, some are never able to deal with it. They are forever marked in their own minds as victims. If you have been the victim of sexual abuse, whether from a family member or someone else, please hear me loud and clear: *It was not your fault.*

Childhood sexual abuse is an act of mistrust—in other words, a violation of trust. Like Cynthia, the victim often loves and trusts the person who is abusing them. Children like the attention they are getting, even though there is something wrong associated with it. That child will grow up having difficulty with double messages in relationships. They will have trouble knowing if they should or shouldn't trust someone.

Usually in cases of incest or assault from a "trusted" adult friend, the perpetrator tells the victim, "Do not tell anybody or I will get in trouble." The child feels they should tell someone but does not want to get the one they love in trouble. And they fear that they, too, will be in trouble. Now the child is in a double bind. They feel guilty about what is taking place, wanting to confess it, yet letting the secret out will get their abuser in trouble. As a result, the child does not say anything and suffers in silence.

When I met Lisa, it didn't take long to discover the source of her pain. No matter how much Lisa wished and dreamed, her family of origin was far from ideal. In her home, everyone was doing their own thing. Her father drank the nights away. Most days, her mother was couchbound due to an addiction to prescription drugs. Feeling unwanted and unloved, Lisa learned to trust no one and to fend for herself.

Unfortunately, she could not fend off a family member who violated her sexually.

The home is supposed to be our safe haven, filled with love and trust. For Lisa, however, the home became a prison, full of hurt and devoid of everything good and healthy a young child needs. She hid the pain of the sexual assault because she didn't know who could help. No one had helped her before.

In response, Lisa developed her own ways of fixing her pain. For years, she perpetuated the illusion that she had it all together. In some ways, Lisa became strong and self-sufficient, driven by a need to survive. Afraid of somebody violating her again, Lisa also became self-protective. All she really wanted was for somebody to love her.

As a young woman, Lisa was drawn to a well-known family in the community. They seemed so together and exuded such a security that Lisa felt they had what she needed. She felt safe. She married the young man of the family. Then one day, this family and the son suddenly moved out of town, abandoning her. That was her first marriage.

Lisa was then on to her second marriage. She married a man who, like her own father, was not there for her. He escaped life through drugs and then affairs. Lisa ended up being the caretaker, the strong one, taking responsibility to fix everything. Again, this reinforced her belief that she could not depend on anyone but herself. As a result, Lisa found it difficult to let anyone close and get to know her.

By the time I met Lisa, her second husband had deserted her for someone else. Lisa's self-image and self-worth were at an all-time low.

While the process has taken a few years, I have seen God heal Lisa's damaged wounds. Many Christian couples in her church have come alongside her to help her and her children. At first it was hard for her to receive from them. Slowly, she began to let go of her fear and allowed others to be there for her.

Through the counseling process, Lisa also gained respect for herself and realized she could expect others to respect her too. She mentioned to me recently that now that she did not have dramas going on—others to rescue and care-take—she didn't know what to fill her life up with. She is at the right place now to allow God to fill her life with the right things and right people. Healing from the trauma of childhood sexual abuse is essential to being able to connect in authentic intimacy in marriage.

One family came to see me because their teenage son was molesting their daughter. It turned out that the mother and the father had been molested when they were young. Neither one of them ever told anybody about it. They never dealt with it, keeping their past a secret. In the process of counseling, I uncovered the fact that all of the children were sexually involved with each other. This is a horrible, devastating instance of the parents' past influencing the lives of their children. Their secret really did not stay hidden and eventually destroyed the family. Incest leaves incredibly deep and serious wounds. If not addressed, the pain will fester and spread like cancer, affecting everyone involved.

I counseled a woman who had grown up in a large family with only one bathroom. Even through their teenage years, all of the children showered in front of each other and their parents.

While there was never any physical violation, this woman, now an adult, had all of the manifestations as if she had been sexually abused. In this type of situation, even though physical contact didn't happen, sexual boundaries were being violated. It is totally inappropriate for older children of the opposite sex, especially teenagers, to be in an environment to view each other's naked bodies.

## Confused Image

Sexual abuse victims begin to believe they must have done something wrong to deserve the abuse. The logical conclusion they reach is "I must be bad." Confusion sets in when they also feel affirmed by the attention they are receiving. This confusion carries over into the arena of their sexual image. These children do not have the ability to discern the different sexual feelings of pleasure and shame. On one hand, the sexual abuse brings them shame. On the other hand, it also generates a premature arousal of their sexual feelings. This leaves the victim with a distorted picture or image of themselves.

Those who have been violated as children will struggle with their self-esteem. Their worth was measured by meeting the sexual needs of their abuser. Often these individuals will become sexually active and promiscuous as young teenagers. Because of the sexual nature of the abuse, they believe they will only get attention through sex. Sometimes, the opposite occurs, where victims will draw back from any sexual situation.

Victims of sexual abuse struggle with confused personal boundaries. They will vacillate between permissive, loose boundaries (it may seem as if they have no boundaries) and strict, rigid boundaries, becoming cold and indifferent.

Often, sexually assaulted women will tell me that during some period in their lives they thought of themselves as a whore. This thinking does not surprise me. Their self-esteem and self-respect had gone down the drain. Sometimes they end up getting married with this poor attitude. They will eventually wonder why they even got married, doubting the kind of person they attracted when they felt so bad about themselves. Having engaged in pre-marital sex only adds to the confusion.

The opposite response is also a very real experience for many individuals. Some people block themselves off from others as a form of protection from ever feeling what they did as children. They find it difficult allowing anyone to get close to them. Consequently, some individuals will downplay and suppress their sexuality. This does not work, because all of us are created with sexuality. The issue is not sexual desires in and of themselves but how they were formed and affected by someone else's abuse.

## A Grip on Control

One devastating aspect of childhood sexual abuse is that the victim has no control over their situation. Any child who has been violated will say "I am never going to put myself in a position to be controlled like that again." To individuals who have made this vow, many times commitment in a relationship is equated as control. Therefore, afraid of being controlled once again, an adult will have a difficult time being intimate with another. They may avoid making any kind of commitment. If they do get married, they will resist totally giving themselves to their spouse. They do not have an innate understanding of a safe, mutually healthy relationship.

Every person, no matter their past, is reluctant to be vulnerable. To experience true intimacy, a couple must get to the point of being so vulnerable they know their partner could hurt them, because we as imperfect humans inevitably hurt one another. This is a scary prospect for anyone, but for those who were violated as children, this situation is downright terrifying. An unhealed victim of childhood sexual abuse will hold onto their power at all costs. What I find so sad is that these individuals could not keep their abusers from violating them, so they keep everyone else at bay, cutting themselves off from healthy, loving relationships.

Many times, I have counseled couples who were experiencing a power struggle. One spouse was in the dark and could not figure out why they were fighting so often. They described their partner as if they were surrounded by a fortress. "They just will not let me in." In reality, that individual was trying to protect him/herself from being out of control. Because of the wounds from their childhood abuse, they erected an emotional barrier to others. It's as if they have hung a sign saying: "You cannot come in. I am not going to let you get close enough to hurt or control me."

As I work with adults of childhood sexual abuse, my purpose is to help them let go of the past, to get to the point to say: "That experience was real and molded me into who I am, but it is not how God created me to be." It takes time to get to this place. The difficulty is in the fact that the abuser exercised assumed authority over the child, and in the most violating offense, in some way represented God to the child.

With a few couples I counseled, a tragic truth eventually surfaced. As children, the men had been violated by someone from church: a staff member, Sunday school teacher, pastor, or priest. These victimizers represented God *and* an authority. Now that's a double whammy!

Naturally, as a result of this abuse, these men rebelled against God at some point in their lives. I could not believe that these men were even willing to talk to me about their pasts. It is a miracle that each one had again begun seeking God. In terms of their relationships with women, they must learn what it means to be intimate. The walls of protection must come down. But the real change will come when they see themselves in the image God made them sexually, not how the violation made them.

Unresolved hurt and pain from incest keep the victim in bondage. A person cannot appropriately bond to another if they are in bondage. Instead, there is a tendency to bond in the wrong way, to the wrong person, or to project bonding in the wrong arena. Bondage actually blinds someone to true bonding.

God created us to bond to Him through His Spirit. He also created us to bond to another human being of the opposite sex. The fear surrounding this bonding keeps a person in bondage. That is why we must deal with the truth and bring our past into the light of Christ.

On the cross, Christ took back what Satan stole from us and the nature we lost when Adam sinned. When a person accepts Christ, God restores his or her identity to its pre-Fall state of perfection—our inner man. For the rest of our lives, we must deal with the distortion of our outer man. That involves taking back what God has given us and is rightfully ours, which sin stole from us. The sinful act of sexual abuse steals from the victim what God had intended them to be and have. The good news is that through Christ's power, the victim can reclaim and take it back.

Thankfully, God doesn't operate like we do with time and space. David Seamands talks about this in his book *Healing for Damaged Emotions*. He describes how there's no time to God. He died for all men—past, present, and future. That means He has broken the power of sin over you, and that includes the power of other people's sins that have affected you as well.

A little girl or a little boy who was violated as a child, can now, as an adult, bring Christ into that wounded place. Today, in the present, healing can occur from the violation that occurred years earlier in childhood. Dan Allender also shares key principles about recovering from childhood sexual abuse and more on this topic in his books *The Wounded Heart: Hope for Adult Victims of Childhood Sexual Abuse* and *Healing the Wounded Heart: The Heartache of Sexual Abuse and the Hope of Transformation*.

When a youth has been sexually violated in any way, intimacy seems to be impossible. I assure you it's not. Healing and intimacy are possible. Stay with me and I'll show you how. If you have lived with the pain of sexual abuse, my goal and desire is to help you discover the image God made you in, not the image that sin molded. To restore your self-respect and dignity, bringing you back more and more to the person God created. Seek Him with your whole heart and let Him bring forgiveness and healing and true intimacy into your heart.

CHAPTER 9

# The Bondage of Barriers

Anyone who has ever tried to know another person—mentally, emotionally, and physically in marriage—has encountered fear. In every relationship, one person's "imperfectness" has hurt or violated the other. Back and forth from one person to the other, the violation of the fear continues. So we build emotional walls and barriers for protection.

We are imperfect people living in an imperfect world. It is inevitable that someone we love—our parents, siblings, friends, or spouse—will hurt us, unintentionally or not. When this happens, the natural tendency is to protect ourselves from being hurt again. As a result, each of us has built some type of wall around our heart. Unfortunately, blocking off part of ourselves to avoid pain will also keep us from connecting and being intimate with anyone else, which results in hurting those who long to be close to us. Also as a result of the pain, many of us have developed mechanisms to protect ourselves. Some of these mechanisms are the strongholds in our lives that trap us in repeating the same failures as we attempt to be intimate. So the cycle continues.

For those who have suffered physical, emotional, or sexual abuse, the walls are higher. In cases like this, however, these walls often serve as protective boundaries and are essential for survival against harmful relationships. There is a big difference between barriers and boundaries.

> *Boundaries are not impenetrable walls used for isolation, extreme self- protection, or obsessive self-control. Boundaries are a necessary part of our healing and growth. Out of respect for ourselves and others, boundaries are used to recognize our limitations and the limitations of other human beings.*

Boundaries are not impenetrable walls used for isolation, extreme self-protection, or obsessive self-control. Most often, boundaries are a necessary part of our healing and growth. Out of respect for ourselves and others, boundaries are used to recognize our limitations and the limitations of other human beings.

Lisa from the previous chapter exercised valuable boundaries in her next relationship. After being abandoned by her second husband, Lisa started dating a man who had never been married. The more time they spent together, she began to realize he was expecting things of her that were not realistic. It became painfully obvious that while Lisa was getting "healthy," her boyfriend was stuck in his own issues, unwilling to get help. Before, she would have taken full responsibility for the relationship. But now she was able to take a stand and set up boundaries out of self-respect. Because she understood what she could or could not be to someone, she confronted her boyfriend and said "No" to meeting his needs. Although it wasn't easy, Lisa knew she needed to break up with him. This was the first time she was the one who ended a relationship.

This is a good example of healthy boundaries.

Walls, on the other hand, construct an emotional prison. Yes, they protect, but they also isolate. Rigid, self-protective walls shut out beneficial, enjoyable relationships. Once the walls go up, the wounded person inside will do everything possible to keep the wall in place and stay inside that wall in bondage. Rather than dealing with the pain, either inside or outside the walls, many wounded people initiate coping mechanisms to deal with life.

## Coping Mechanisms

Adults have told me they have no idea why they are behaving a certain way. As I work with them, the answer becomes clear. In childhood, they created a way of being safe and secure. In order to control their world, they developed coping mechanisms.

No family is perfect, so in a sense, all of us have developed mechanisms of protection to some degree. But as we've already covered, there is a wide range of experiences that cause pain. Some are quite a bit more severe than others—emotional, physical, or sexual abuse; abandonment; emotional incest. The more extreme the abuse, the stronger the coping mechanism the victim puts in place. There are several typical coping behaviors in children who have suffered from these more intense sources of pain.

Previously easygoing children begin acting out. They start hitting others for seemingly no reason. Other children may get extremely nervous or upset in the presence of other children in a disagreement. Some children will begin to ritualistically repeat certain behaviors to ease compulsive thoughts, potentially evolving into full-blown obsessive-compulsive disorder. As we've already seen with Valerie and others, some children will become master caretakers of others, trying to fix everything. Usually, this behavior causes them to neglect their own needs. In the face of pain, some children just decide not to think about it. They enter into complete denial. Their reasoning is that if they do not deal with it they will not remember it, so it will not hurt. Many children simply withdraw. They become sullen and quiet, isolating themselves from friends and activities they used to enjoy.

For a child in pain, these coping mechanisms are necessary for survival. These methods are essential for the child to control their world. Self-defense mechanisms such as these, no matter how unhealthy at the time, enable the child to function in their young life.

Then the child moves into adulthood. And guess what? They bring their coping mechanisms right along with them. While these defense mechanisms may seem to work for a while, they are not healthy patterns for a sustainable good life. Inevitably, opposition hits the coping mechanisms too hard, and they don't work like they used to. The adult who had depended on childhood coping skills may start having trouble in their relationships, at work, or with their children, and they are no longer able to cope.

The very mechanisms they used as children to help them endure are now the mechanisms that are keeping them from being intimate, blocking them from being free to be themselves. What once was a means to survival is now an element of destruction.

Adults who acted out as children become bullies as adults, sometimes repeating the pattern as abusive parents themselves. Children who ease their pain through OCD patterns as children may continue to ritualistically repeat certain behaviors to ease their obsessive thoughts as adults. Caretakers morph into martyrs. Some adults continue to busy themselves taking care of others while neglecting their own needs. Denial sets up a still-wounded adult to live in fantasy, unwilling to face the reality of life. Adults in denial refuse to acknowledge they have even been hurt. In order to do this, they shut off part of themselves and may become hardened. And if a child continues to withdraw, patterns of isolation will cause that same adult to block themselves off from those closest to them. For an adult, workaholism is a classic isolating behavior.

If not addressed, defense mechanisms continue to evolve beyond childhood coping skills. Some adults use sex—from abstinence to permissiveness—as a means to control their pain or even other people. Some adults cannot face the truth of their painful lives and literally run away. Others may just escape in alcohol or drugs. Some adults use food to change their emotional mood, a destructive mechanism that shows up in eating disorders as early as teen years.

Charles, in his early sixties, came to see me after hitting rock bottom. He had just spent a week in a hospital drying out, but this was not his first time. For decades, alcohol abuse had been ruining his life.

The first time Charles and I talked, he shared something he had kept bottled up for years. He says talking about it was the key that opened the door for him. Charles says, "I was finally able to tell the truth about my father's death." He discovered there was a background of mental health problems in his family that had remained hidden.

When Charles was just sixteen, his father died. But Charles's pain began long before his father's death. As a child, Charles never felt loved by his father. No matter the length of time they spent together, something was missing. He could never feel close to his father. His father had extreme mood swings, constantly in fear of someone following him. Although he never received treatment, Charles believes his father was schizophrenic. This left Charles without knowing the healthy intimacy between father and son, which impacted his ability to be intimate with his wife as an adult. With no connection or transparency in his family system, Charles felt unloved and unaccepted, ultimately unable to love others.

Like so many wounded children in situations similar to Charles's, he turned to food to fill the emptiness he felt. Comfort food became his escape. As a result, his childhood overeating turned into a life-long struggle. Early on, Charles acquired another pain killer: humor. "Looking back, humor was my immune system. I developed humor to have people want me around."

Charles's father was a social drinker. But whenever he drank, he became extremely verbally abusive. During one explosive binge, Charles locked his angry father in his room until he finally passed out. The next morning, everyone behaved as if nothing had happened. The incident was brushed under the rug like all the others.

It was in college that Charles married his high school sweetheart, Nadia. After graduation, he was on his way in a new career. He was also on his way to becoming an alcoholic. His job required him to travel during the week, with visits home on the weekends. This left him little time to spend with his young wife and, within a few years, two little boys. To ease the boredom and loneliness of the road, Charles began drinking.

The years went by quickly. Charles cannot remember how or when his drinking got out of hand. He never thought he had a problem. But when he started to take a quick shot in the morning before his coffee, he wondered if maybe something was not right. Still, he kept drinking … and drinking. A couple of times, Charles went into the hospital to dry out, only to return to the bottle.

Then Charles hit bottom and hit it hard. He lost his job. He just could not keep depression at bay this time. "I was drinking myself to death. Then everything crashed in on me. I could not and did not want to get out of bed." When Nadia came to his bedside and asked him if he wanted help, he numbly replied, "Yes."

Once again, Charles visited the hospital, but this stay would be his last. It was then that he began counseling with me. "The worst thing people go through is not talking about their pain. With Gene, I was able to do that." As Charles confronted his pain, he did not need alcohol anymore. He now has no desire to drink at all.

Charles would never have guessed the change in his relationship with Nadia. "During all of those years of traveling, there was a strain in our marriage. It was all my fault. I was horrible when I was drinking. After I gave up alcohol for good, I asked Nadia why she did not leave me. I will never forget her answer, 'Because I love you.' She has been incredible. We spend a lot of time together now, talking about anything."

Through counseling and his wife's patient love, Charles was able to replace his coping mechanisms of food, humor, and alcohol with God's better design.

Another coping mechanism I see frequently is people pleasing: doing whatever it takes to fit in, to be accepted. The danger with this method is that people allow themselves to be controlled from the outside. No one else should have that much power over who we are. But it happens all the time. Let's revisit Cynthia. She developed her own coping mechanisms after being dismissed by her father and sexually abused by a church member. She began looking for love, no matter the cost.

As Cynthia reached adolescence, she still felt the need for love and acceptance. "I continued to struggle with feeling pretty, fun, or smart enough. I attended a youth group at church and did whatever they did because I wanted to be accepted. With every new person I met and new situation I encountered, I would try to figure out how to make that person like and accept me. In high school, I began to date and started drinking with my friends."

In these dating relationships, Cynthia blossomed. Her feelings of inadequacy and fear vanished in the presence of young men. When she was eighteen, she had intercourse for the first time. This began a long string of relationships.

Cynthia used sex to gain acceptance. "I felt that I was able to connect on an emotional level with most of the young men I dated. But the truth was, I was involved in many inappropriate relationships. The men I dated were verbally abusive, demeaning, and disrespectful toward me."

After graduating from college, Cynthia started a good job with a large company. Her feelings of not being good enough followed her there. "I would do anything job-related that I was asked. I wanted to ensure that my boss liked me. I thought if I did a good job, I would feel accepted. I worked hard and was quickly recognized for it. Finally, I was able to achieve and feel some level of acceptance. Although I still worried that someday they would discover how incompetent I really was."

At the workplace, Cynthia met James. "We dated and I decided he was Mr. Right. My parents really liked him, and although I did not feel in love with him, he seemed like the perfect provider and very stable. We got married and did everything together. But I still did not feel 'in love' in my marriage. My old feelings of fear and inadequacy began to return."

Sadly, marriage did not give Cynthia acceptance and love the way she wanted it. "I was still searching for the love and acceptance I felt was missing in my family. I constantly felt pulled to look for acceptance outside my marriage. I continued to be more concerned with how people accepted me or approved of my actions."

James was different from all the other men Cynthia had dated. He never treated her like they had. He loved and respected her. But sex with James just was not as exciting as in other relationships. The emotional closeness she felt with other men was missing also. It was after they married that it became a real problem. With time, Cynthia did not want to have sex with James at all. She felt disgusted. James felt rejected. There was no intimacy—physical or emotional—in their relationship.

As a result, Cynthia created a fantasy world and James got into pornography. Both had developed coping mechanisms of having affairs in their minds. They were looking to something outside their relationship to get their needs met. But they only succeeded in creating false intimacy, which left them feeling empty. There was no denying something was missing in their relationship.

"I had an ideal in my head of how James should act in every situation with me, and, of course, he could never measure up. I continued talking to a few of my old boyfriends on the phone and ended up betraying James."

Cynthia admits her self-worth was wrapped up in gaining acceptance through emotional and physical intimacy. And when things were not working with James, she was deeply troubled. James insisted something was wrong too. More than anything, they wanted their marriage to work. They hoped that the problems would somehow fix themselves. When that did not happen, they sought professional help. After seeing numerous counselors, Cynthia and James came to me.

We explored childhood wounds and coping mechanisms, beginning the process toward healing.

## Recognizing the Conditions

Cynthia's sexuality was learned in the context of shame. She associated feelings of love and acceptance with her sexual abuse. She felt good in the inappropriate relationship with her grandfatherly friend from church. As a young woman, she became quite promiscuous and chose men who disrespected her. The coping mechanism of sex gave her the feeling of being in control. The inappropriate relationships felt right and normal to her. There was a mystique, an excitement to having sex outside of marriage. And when Cynthia got married, the excitement ended.

God designed marriage as the relationship where sex is appropriate and good. It is supposed to be the right place to experience sexuality. There is to be no shame in the marriage bed. But Cynthia did feel shame. It is said that shame (painful feeling of guilt for improper behavior) leads to contempt (loathing of self, others, or God). Cynthia began to despise James.

Cynthia was confused by her contradictory feelings. Where she was supposed to feel good, she felt bad. And where she was supposed to feel bad, she felt good. To dismantle Cynthia's coping mechanisms, she was going to need to process the pain behind them.

## Processing the Pain

It was not until we were well into the counseling process that Cynthia was finally able to acknowledge that something was wrong with the abuse she had endured. All of these years, she felt that it was "no big deal," a classic symptom of denial. But the abuse was affecting every decision she made. To Cynthia, love was defined as what she had experienced at the hands of her molester. Then, as a woman, the only love she knew was through sex.

Whenever we talked about sex, Cynthia had no "bad" feelings or thoughts associated with it. She was totally de-sensitized to any embarrassment or shame about sex—inappropriate sex, that is. It all went back to the abuse.

As we talked about the molestation, I confronted Cynthia. "I cannot believe that you didn't feel something as that man was doing those things to you."

It turns out, Cynthia did feel shameful at first. But this was the father figure who was nice and accepted her. As a six-year-old girl, she assumed the treatment she received from this "kind" man was okay, because she thought he loved her. And she needed love and acceptance.

Even before Cynthia met her abuser, she felt it was not safe in her family. Safety was found outside the family. This most likely contributed to her being susceptible to the overtures of her abuser. She never experienced intimacy in her family. Again, she found intimacy outside her family. In reality though, the intimacy she found was only a false intimacy.

The pattern for little Cynthia was set: Safety and intimacy were to be found outside the family. Cynthia transferred those feelings to her marriage. She was drawn to meet her needs outside her relationship with James, relying on old coping skills to attract extra-marital affairs.

At first, Cynthia had no idea how distorted her image was or how tightly she clung to her coping mechanisms; she was so far in the darkness. Then she began reading her Bible and going to church. Cynthia says, "I finally understood that God was not waiting for me to do something acceptable that would make me good enough for salvation. There was nothing I could do to earn that salvation. So I received Jesus into my heart." In this new relationship, Cynthia was able to begin seeing herself through God's eyes. He gave her the power to change her thinking and to begin retraining her senses.

Cynthia was very uncomfortable as she began making changes. First, she had to stop fantasizing and thinking she had to go outside her marriage to be accepted. She had to learn that her worth was not wrapped up in sex; her value was not in her body. This truth is especially difficult for someone who has been sexually abused to grasp.

I helped Cynthia learn to not be a victim to her feelings. When she felt a certain way—guilt, for instance—I asked her what she was thinking (sex with her husband was disgusting). Then, I had her think and determine where this thought came from. I asked, "Who told you that you should be guilty?" In this example, she was able to trace her thoughts to sex with James as being shameful to the distorted image she developed through the improper sexual relationship with her abuser.

When she became aware of what she was thinking and where it came from, she was able to reject it and replace it with the truth.

This became a process we repeated over and over. At first, it was quite difficult for Cynthia to give up what she had spent a lifetime being familiar with. When she tried to change her thinking and bring it into the light, her feelings almost seemed to scream, "No! This isn't right!" But over time, her feelings rebelled less and less. As Cynthia embraced the truth about herself, she experienced freedom to be the woman God created her to be.

Even now, there are times when Cynthia's old coping mechanisms pull on her. She feels responsible for others' emotional responses, and she struggles with looking for her acceptance from the world. At those times, she must take her thoughts captive to the One who loves her unconditionally and gives her total acceptance. This will be a process that she will repeat, prayerfully less and less, the rest of her life.

Through Christ's power, Cynthia is able to love herself as God loves her. Out of this newfound love, she can give herself unreservedly (with no shame or guilt) to James. She is no longer in bondage to giving herself physically to get love. Cynthia has come out from behind her wall and is now truly free to be herself with James. She says, "I now see that I had not married the wrong man but that I had the wrong expectations, and I was hiding behind the same coping mechanisms I'd adopted as a little girl. After many months of praying for our marriage to be as God designed and looking to Scripture for answers, God has created true intimacy between James and me. This intimacy that used to somehow elude me has now become so real to me that I can barely remember not having it with James. We have learned how to communicate with acceptance and love."

Cynthia opened herself to God and to outside help. Once held captive by hidden shame and fierce coping mechanisms, she finally was able to replace her protective wall with trust in God. Not only is she now enjoying a life of authentic intimacy with her husband, but she also is experiencing healing to a wound that goes way back.

"I now rely on God to fill my need for acceptance. God has become my Father, my Comforter, and my Provider. Because I now look to God as my Father who meets my needs, I have been able to forgive my dad. A little over a year ago, I was able to work up the courage to meet with my dad. I had serious doubts about whether this was a good idea. My old fears and feelings of inadequacy resurfaced with a vengeance. But I know God wanted me to face this fear and trust Him to help me through it. I did, and the meeting with my dad went very well. We were able to be truthful, honest, and loving. I had prayed that God would allow me to approach Dad as Jesus would, to forgive and love him. I was able for the first time to understand his troubled childhood. God has created a new relationship for my dad and me. I know none of this would have been possible without Jesus in my life."

The mechanisms we develop as children to cope with our pain hinder God from working in our lives. Cynthia could have chosen to hang onto her coping mechanisms for dear life. She was legitimately abused as an innocent child and had every right to feel the things she did. Thankfully, Cynthia made the courageous choice to come out from behind her protective wall and face the truth. That is where she found healing and intimacy within her marriage.

As we bring this section to a close, I want to reassure you: No wall is too high or too thick, no defense mechanism too strong, no shame too great to keep you captive in old patterns. God promises to always be there for you. If you let Him, He will heal you His way—the perfect way. God desires for you to be healthy, full of life, and free—in Him and in your marriage. Intimacy awaits!

*No wall is too high or too thick, no defense mechanism too strong, no shame too great to keep you captive in old patterns.*

# Part Three

Moving Through the Pain of
Severed Connection

## CHAPTER 10

# Affairs—Nothing Fair About Them

I RECEIVED A call from Julia. Her story is typical of so many people I have counseled. Change the circumstances, shift the characters, and alter the details, but the pain from being betrayed is always the same.

Devastated and broken, Julia had just found out that her husband was having an affair.

Adultery is perhaps the most disastrous attack on intimacy in marriage. Considering the 3-D nature of our beings, as we've already discussed, unfaithfulness violates intimacy in marriage in every way possible—mental, emotional, and physical. When the adulterer goes outside the marriage for physical satisfaction, emotional and mental connection with their spouse has been tarnished. Like I said earlier: The soul knows when it isn't connecting, and that disconnection is painful.

The pain of betrayal is deep, like none other. Victims trusted their marriage partner and gave their life to them, then the offending spouse took advantage of that trust and betrayed the loyal one, manifesting a pain so deep the victim wonders if they will survive. If this has happened to you, you know what I mean. The pain of betrayal cuts right to the depth of your soul. Stunned, a betrayed spouse pleads for answers: "Why would someone I care about do this to me?"

## The Reason for Affairs

Affairs are a process of deterioration. Rarely are they an impulsive decision. The affair is a symptom of a greater problem.

Most people get into affairs because they are emotionally bankrupt, not because of physical temptation. They have an emotional need that is not being met by their spouse. But some husbands or wives get into affairs because of problems with their self-image. My affairs were due to my own need for power. My unfaithfulness to Eldeen had nothing to do with her. Which is why I say there's nothing fair about affairs. They can happen for many reasons.

The people I have counseled did not plan on having an affair, but the conditions were right, and most importantly, they were vulnerable. Vulnerability to affairs begins when one in the marriage is disappointed or dissatisfied, even if the unfaithful spouse doesn't know exactly why. Every relationship will have problems, but if conflict is avoided or unresolved, the door is wide open to seeking another person to meet their needs.

If a couple does not deal with unresolved conflict or a lack of intimacy, they are in danger of diverting their attention from one object of devotion to another. This isn't necessarily another adult. Often when I ask people where their marriage went wrong, they point back to having their first child. While the new mother devotes more of her attention to the child, the father may get more involved at the office. He gets affirmation from work, and she gets affirmation from nurturing her child. Their relationship begins to suffer.

I caution people who are disgruntled with their spouse to be careful who they share their problems with. It is dangerous to turn to a member of the opposite sex. If that person is married, too, and begins to share his or her problems, you will sense an identity with each other over your common problems. This connection is nothing more than a false intimacy, an emotional affair.

*If a couple does not deal with unresolved conflict or a lack of intimacy, they are in danger of diverting their attention from one object of devotion to another.*

The path to a sexual affair continues when a person begins to fantasize what it would be like being with another person. The fantasy only creates an unrealistic expectation of what they could have in this "new" relationship compared to what they have in their marriage.

Sexual addictions can also lead to affairs. Men, and even some women, who are addicted to pornography or other aspects of a sexual addiction, are living in a fantasy world. Any spouse of a sex addict will tell you they cannot compete with a fantasy.

Unresolved childhood wounds also can lead to unfaithfulness in a marriage. Belief systems get twisted, causing a spouse to "need" something different than what their spouse is able to deliver. Patterns of lying, justifying, and rationalizing also open the door to the deception of having an affair.

When a spouse is unfaithful in marriage, they are violating more than their wedding vows. They are violating God's priorities. Loyalty is tops on God's list of priorities.

> Unresolved childhood wounds also can lead to unfaithfulness in a marriage. Belief systems get twisted, causing a spouse to "need" something different than what their spouse is able to deliver.

When Jesus was asked which was the greatest commandment, He responded: " 'Love the Lord your God with all your heart and with all your soul and with all your mind.' This is the first and greatest commandment" (Matthew 22:37–38). It is also a loyalty statement. In other words, will you be loyal to God above all other things?

Life is out of order because of sin. From the get-go, our priorities are not in order because we are born in the wake of Adam and Eve's disobedience. Although we have been made in God's image, we are not automatically loyal to Him. I have been known to comment, tongue-in-cheek, that if our culture continues as it is going, it will not be long until the word "loyalty" is removed from the dictionary.

It is God's loyalty to us—demonstrated in the sacrificial act of His Son—and allowing Him to live through us, that enables us to be loyal. When a person has an affair, their priorities of loyalties are out of order. First, they have been disloyal to God. Next, they have been disloyal to themselves, violating their own identity that has been created in the image of God. Finally, they have been disloyal to their spouse. The betrayer has taken the loyalty they pledged to their spouse and given it to another. Adultery is nothing more than stealing.

## Through the Betrayal

During my conversation with Julia, I highlighted the path I take people through who are dealing with the betrayal of their spouse. It is not a quick trip and it is far from easy.

I told Julia I didn't want to give her quick, pat answers. Julia considers herself a Christian and didn't want to leave the relationship. I agreed with her on not jumping out of her marriage so quickly. I validated her pain, acknowledging the fact that her husband's betrayal is extremely painful. Then I explained to her that if I was her counselor, I would help her walk through the pain and help her understand how to approach her situation in a way that she could say, "I have done all God wanted me to do."

When I asked Julia if she or her husband were seeing a counselor, she told me she had suggested counseling, but so far her husband has refused to go. And although he claimed it was over with the woman he was having the affair with, he told Julia he wants to continue having flings. To me, that sounds like an adulterer who doesn't want to change.

Julia is wondering how long she should tolerate his adulterous behavior. They are not separated, still living in the same house. Julia is trying to be loving, understanding, and supportive, but she asked me, "How much of this do I have to put up with before I say enough is enough?" Very carefully, I told Julia that God would never ask her to submit to a lie to bring about a truth.

Understand what I am saying. We cannot continue to live in a lie forever without it destroying us. Somewhere along the line, we have to draw a healthy boundary versus blocking ourselves off behind a defensive wall to protect ourselves. God wants us safe, but He doesn't want us sequestered in hiding. As Christians, we can set boundaries out of self-respect and respect for our spouse. I shared with Julia, "If you do not come to the point of setting a self-respecting boundary, the sin done to you will harden you so much you will get bitter, and it will destroy you. You need to set a boundary before you get to that point."

> *God wants us safe, but He doesn't want us sequestered in hiding.*

A boundary in this situation needs to require the adulterer to make a choice. A spouse who has been betrayed by adultery, with no sign of change, cannot live with that sin and continue to be sinned against, dreamily thinking the unfaithful spouse will somehow respond differently. That is not realistic, and it's not safe. If your spouse has threatened to leave the marriage if you don't allow affairs, and you hold no boundaries to the contrary in place, your spouse could use your conviction of not wanting a divorce to continue their sinful lifestyle.

Before you set a boundary, however, whatever it may be, you need to know where you are in your heart. Make sure your heart is right before God and trust Him to help you know how to set a boundary confidently and securely. Surrender your fears to God about what your unfaithful spouse might do, so your fears will not control you.

Julia confessed to me her biggest problem—the fear of being alone and starting her life over again at the age of forty. She wanted to keep her family together for their daughter's sake. Julia was not the product of divorce, although her parents fought a lot until her mother died when Julia was twelve. Her husband's parents were divorced. Both come from dysfunctional backgrounds with fathers who were alcoholics. Julia's husband was rebellious as a child, and he is still rebellious as an adult. Julia figured she was going to be the one to save him from himself. She even warned him this affair was going to happen, because she could see it coming, and he did not listen.

I quickly recognized Julia's second biggest problem: She wanted to fix her husband. She felt guilty about abandoning him, believing he was confused. In her love, she wanted to do the right thing by him. I understand this dilemma so well. Countless clients sit in my office wishing, hoping, wanting to do everything they can to get their adulterous spouse to change. Julia had been trying to fix her husband for eight years. At the end of our call, Julia agreed to see a counselor in her area, since we did not live in the same state. I affirmed her for taking the step to work on herself and letting God work on her husband.

None of us can fix our wandering spouse. We must give them up to the Lord and quit trying to fix the problems within them. Let God deal with them in His way.

That's the point Eldeen had to get to with me after I confessed my unfaithfulness to her.

### *Eldeen*

Before Gene became a Christian and ended his adulterous lifestyle, there were times I went to my favorite spot on the lake and questioned my sanity for staying in the marriage. I knew adultery was a biblical reason for divorce. But I could not deny that God told me to stay. Oh yes, I argued with God many times about the unjust situation in my marriage. Then I would get confirmation through the Holy Spirit, His Word, and circumstances that I was not to leave or run away—I was to stay and fight for my marriage.

After Gene went on another business trip and stopped off in Las Vegas, I was so angry. I went to the lake to blow off steam and "talk" with God. I was ready to withdraw all of our money from the bank and take off. To heck with my commitment. To heck with what I thought God was leading me to do. I just did not deserve this kind of treatment. I was so hurt.

Instead, I took my pain and anger, my worry and resentment to Jesus. When I did, my circumstances did not change, but I began to. For the first time in my life, I could forgive Gene because Jesus forgave me, and I knew He could forgive Gene through me. I couldn't do it, but Jesus could. I asked God to help me be the wife He wanted me to be. Of course, I asked God to change Gene too. But I was responsible for me; God had to work on Gene.

I know this is an excruciating task, to surrender and forgive when you have been so betrayed. I also know it is the only way for you to have peace. When you surrender yourself and your unfaithful spouse to God, you never know exactly how God will work.

You cannot control your spouse, but you can decide who and what is controlling you. That is where the help comes in if you are getting counsel. I have dealt with this kind of situation dozens and dozens of times. I cannot guarantee the end result, but I can assure you of the peace you will have when you know you have done all that God wanted you to do.

## Facing the Truth

Frequently a client will say to me, "I think my spouse is having an affair. What should I do?" When it comes to facing the truth, let me begin by saying suspicions definitely need to be confronted. Burying doubts under the rug and hoping they will go away just will not work. However, I advise doing some preparation before the confrontation takes place. As I've said before: Truth is never optional; timing and method are.

> As I've said before: Truth is never optional; timing and method are.

When it comes to handling confrontation in the right way, most people need help to prepare themselves emotionally. More problems can be created if someone responds out of their hurt and rejection by attacking back or running away. If you suspect your spouse may be having an affair, I encourage you to speak with a counselor or a trusted pastor. You don't need to walk this path alone.

Next, spend some time in prayer. As difficult as it is, give control of the entire situation over to God. Ask Him to help you be ready to deal with the truth. Then I suggest you take thirty days and pray for the truth to be revealed. Almost every time someone has done that, the truth comes out.

While I am a therapist, I am not your therapist. You may want to consider finding one to support you. But I do not suggest hiring a private detective. You do not go looking for the lie to find the truth. You do not go looking in the darkness to find the light. When you start focusing on the light and the truth, the lie will be revealed. Ask Jesus to be the revealer of lies in your marriage. He wants the sin exposed.

> *Do not go looking for the lie to find the truth. Do not go looking in the darkness to find the light. When you start focusing on the light and the truth, the lie will be revealed. Ask Jesus to be the revealer of lies in your marriage. He wants the sin exposed.*

The other reason I do not think it is best to hire a private detective is the potential damage from seeing the actual information that is discovered. Our culture revels in digging up the dirt. The dirtier the better. But once a person has learned all the gory details, they have to live with them. Photographs only make it worse. The details are hard to forget, which makes the healing process more difficult.

My caution in all of this is when you pray for your spouse to come face-to-face with truth, God will answer. His Word, His truth, will not return back to God empty, without accomplishing His desire (Isaiah 55:11). We can be assured that He wants all men and women to come to the truth (2 Peter 3:9). But how your spouse responds to the truth is another matter. They may not respond in the way that you hope. Again, you cannot control another person. You can only take responsibility for yourself and how you respond. If your spouse doesn't respond in repentance and surrender to God, you might need to let them go. If you stay in a marriage with an unfaithful spouse, you will be staying in a lie and that will destroy you. God does not call you to live a lie the rest of your life. There is no intimacy in that.

Whatever happens, keep walking with the Lord. He will help you through it. "So do not fear, for I am with you; do not be dismayed, for I am your God. I will strengthen you and help you; I will uphold you with my righteous right hand" (Isaiah 41:10).

In times of distress, like learning your spouse has been unfaithful to you, the safest place for you to go is the heart of God. So many people have found a rich new intimacy with Jesus in the depth of their brokenness. When your spouse betrays you, God's faithfulness becomes ever more precious. He is faithful to you and loves you with a love that never ceases.

### Eldeen

There were many more difficult times in our marriage that I was tempted to leave. During one horrible, hot summer, among other things, I broke my foot and the dog had mange. It was six months later that Gene came to Christ.

As I look back, I am extremely grateful for the husband and the marriage God has given me. It has been worth ten times—no, a hundred times—over every tear I shed. You may be wondering what made the difference; how did I do it?

Yes, I trusted God and persevered in those incredibly difficult early years. But it was once I really grasped the depth and the height and the love with which God loved me that I had a new freedom in my life to extend to my husband, my family, and my friends. It was totally remarkable to me. In light of Gene's unfaithfulness to me, Christ became a reality. Each and every day I had a decision to make: Would I allow God to control me through Christ? I could cope because God's total faithfulness was more than abundant.

## CHAPTER 11

# Responding to Betrayal

G OD REDEFINES what it means to love Him when we go through situations where one who loves us on a human level betrays us. Betrayal shakes us up to the point where we have to ask ... What does it mean to love? To love God, to love another person, to even love ourself?

Spouses on either side of the betrayal have been disrespected by the act. A common feeling is one of not being worth anything. This is true for both the adulterer and the spouse who has been betrayed. It is at these times that we need to know, really know, God loves us. Some individuals find it difficult to let God love them. They can actually cancel out His love because they feel they were never enough. They may continue to reject, rather than receive, God's love as enough for them in the situations in life.

On both sides of an affair, there is deep pain, but it affects the victim and the offender quite differently. Each is asking different questions on the path to restoration.

## The Victim

Just as there are different mechanisms we develop to cope with childhood pain, there are negative coping responses to betrayal in marriage. More than anything, you want the pain to stop.

To some degree, any hurt turns to anger. We respond to pain, whether emotional or physical, almost automatically. In essence, anger is a natural response to pain, and it happens at the slightest provocation. We've all experienced the onset of irritation when we are hungry or not feeling well. Greater levels of anger arise when we feel threatened or rejected. When we suffer loss, one of the first signs of our grief is anger. Anger is almost always triggered by feelings of pain, whatever the cause.

If we do not feel angry at some point, we are living in denial. And if we do not properly grieve our hurt but let our anger simmer, it can quickly boil over into bitterness, resentment, revenge, and finally, victimization. Rather than easing the pain, this response will destroy a person.

Many people who have been betrayed by their spouse go out and do the same thing. They want to give back the same pain that they received. "I am just going to do it to him so he can know how it feels." I don't know anyone who has been betrayed by their spouse who hasn't had this thought go through their mind. But those who act on this tit-for-tat response do not cancel out their pain—they only increase it. I term this response "recycling." This happens when the wounded spouse covers up the disloyalty in their marriage and seeks another person to overcome the hurt. Often this new relationship is forged in nothing more than manipulation.

Many years ago, a woman came to me because her husband left her. She quickly got involved with another man. Now that relationship is in trouble. As she is sitting in my office, she confesses, "I never should have done that." She hadn't healed the pain from her first marriage. Instead, she tried to fix it by quickly finding another person. If you do not deal with the pain of the betrayal, get some help reconciling who you are and where you are, you are going to do the same thing again wherever you go. You can change the characters in a play, but you've got the same script.

Some victims of adultery withdraw and isolate themselves. As a protective measure, they wall themselves off and don't allow people in. I have heard people say, "I will never let anyone hurt me ever again." Isolation is toxic because we are all born with a need for relationships. Deny that need for too long and depression, or worse, will most likely result.

Attempting to ease the pain, a person may react in many negative ways in dealing with disloyalty. These are our human efforts to fix the pain our own way, but these choices only lead to more pain. There is another response a person can make in the midst of their hurt and pain—turn to God and allow Him to meet your needs His way.

That doesn't mean recovering from betrayal is easy or

without challenges. During the healing process, the question most on the mind of the victim of an affair is "Can I trust you again?" The betrayal spawns more questions: "I do not deserve this. It is not fair. How could this person do this to me?" I hear these questions over and over when I counsel those who have been betrayed. It's always hard to try and answer these questions.

But I do know that God can use their betrayal to strengthen their loyalty to God. Through forgiveness they can let go of their hurt, stopping it from controlling them. The one who has been betrayed can identify with Christ more at this point than at any other time in their life.

"I want to know Christ—yes, to know the power of his resurrection and participation in his sufferings, becoming like him in his death" (Philippians 3:10). I do not understand the fullness of what Christ went through on the cross and the betrayal He suffered at the hands of the people He had created. None of us can say we are totally innocent. But Jesus was absolutely sinless. He never did anything wrong to deserve the treatment He received. Jesus sacrificed Himself on the cross for everyone—including those who betrayed Him.

In any pain, especially betrayal, Christ knows exactly what we are going through. We cannot begin to fathom. I have literally seen a transformation when victims have come before God and allowed Christ to teach them, and they have learned to identify with Him in the midst of their betrayal and experience what He experienced.

When you have been hurt in this way, the pain does not magically disappear. Over time, a physical wound will stop bleeding and heal over. The pain lessens, leaving a scar as a reminder of the trauma. I think our emotional wounds heal in somewhat the same way. The betrayal of a loved one leaves an emotional scar. There will be times when the memory surfaces. That is when you take the pain again to God. In the transaction of giving Him your pain, He will give you a deeper understanding of His love for you. Christ broke the power of that pain and the power of that betrayal over you.

## The Offender

The betrayers ask themselves different questions: "Do I know how to really love somebody? Can somebody love me?"

We will find the answers as we look at Jesus' response to one who betrayed Him. The story begins in John 13. While Jesus and the disciples were observing the Lord's Supper, Jesus predicted his betrayal by one of the disciples. The disciples were stunned, and their confusion only increased when Jesus announced: "My children, I will be with you only a little longer. You will look for me, and just as I told the Jews, so I tell you now: Where I am going, you cannot come" (vs. 33).

Jesus went on to give them a new command. But judging by Peter's response, the disciples were still reeling from the news that Jesus was leaving and could not focus on Jesus' teaching. "Simon Peter asked him, 'Lord where are you going?' Jesus replied, 'Where I am going, you cannot follow now, but you will follow later' " (vs. 36). With emotions running high, Peter asked, "Lord, why can't I follow you now? I will lay down my life for you"(vs. 37). I believe Peter, as enthusiastic as ever, meant what he said with every fiber of his being.

What Jesus said next probably left Peter feeling as if he had been punched in the stomach. "Then Jesus answered, 'Will you really lay down your life for me? I tell you the truth, before the rooster crows, you will disown me three times!' " (vs. 38). That's a painful, penetrating revelation. And it was so true.

Later in the chapter, we read that Jesus was arrested and taken to appear before the high priest. Peter and another disciple had followed Jesus and were waiting in the courtyard. Twice Peter was asked if he was one of the disciples. Both times, Peter replied, "I am not." Then someone recognized him and challenged Peter, "Didn't I see you with Jesus in the olive grove?" Again, Peter denied it. At that very moment, a rooster began to crow.

Would a man who loved Jesus so much that he pledged to lay down his life for Jesus betray Him? Not in a million years. But betray Him he did. Anyone who has betrayed someone they loved knows what Peter must have felt like after disowning Jesus.

Fast forward to the Sea of Galilee, where the disciples were fishing. Jesus had been crucified and resurrected and had already appeared before the disciples twice. On this occasion, the disciples were fishing and had no luck. The next morning, Jesus was on the beach, but the disciples did not recognize Him. Jesus told them to throw the net over the right side of the boat to get a catch. I could just imagine them thinking: *The left side, the right side—it does not matter. There just are not any fish. But what could it hurt one more time?* So they did. The catch was so big they couldn't pull it into the boat. Yeah, now they recognized Jesus. Peter was so excited to see Him, he couldn't wait until the boat reached shore; he jumped into the water and rushed to Jesus.

When they finished eating breakfast, Jesus turned to Peter:

> "Simon, son of John, do you truly love me more than these?"
>
> "Yes, Lord," he said, "you know that I love you."
>
> Jesus said, "Feed my lambs."
>
> Again Jesus said, "Simon, son of John, do you truly love me?"
>
> He answered, "Yes, Lord, you know that I love you."
>
> Jesus said, "Take care of my sheep."
>
> The third time he said to him, "Simon, son of John, do you love me?"
>
> Peter was hurt because Jesus asked him the third time, "Do you love me?" He said, "Lord, you know all things; you know that I love you."
>
> Jesus said, "Feed my sheep" (John 21:15–17).

Three times Peter had denied the Lord. And now three times Jesus asked Peter, "Do you love me?" I don't know a more penetrating question. Could you imagine if Jesus was standing in front of you right now, looking you in the eye, and asking, "Do you love me?" How would you answer Him?

As humans, we are limited in our understanding of unconditional love. Here, Peter had betrayed Jesus and He asks Peter, "Do you love me?" "Of course, I love you," Peter responds. In this interaction, Jesus knew exactly what He was doing to Peter. He was restoring him. Jesus was saying, "Peter, I have forgiven you. I love you. I love you unconditionally, even though you betrayed me."

Sooner or later, the offender must deal with God. He knows full well everything you have done and He knows how rotten you feel. Just like He knew the guilt and shame Adam and Eve were dealing with in the garden after their disobedience, He also knows what you're dealing with. And here's the deal ... God covers your sin with His grace. "Grace teaches us that the most important thing about us is not what we do but who and whose we are in Christ," says Ken Boa, author, teacher, and president of Reflections Ministries.[11] As a forgiven child of God, He guides us in His grace as well. "The biblical doctrine of grace humbles us without degrading us, and elevates us without inflating us."[12] Understanding our nature of "human depravity and human dignity," God brings healing into our humility. He is a God of restoration.

You cannot make up for the hurt you caused. You cannot fix yourself or the one you hurt. But you can receive the unconditional love of God. That is the beginning of restoring your priority of loyalty back to God.

Restoring the relationship with your spouse will also need some serious attention. Restoration in a marriage where betrayal has entered does not happen automatically.

## Dealing with Consequences

As with any sin, there will be inevitable consequences to betrayal that need to be dealt with. The consequences to sin aren't eliminated after you're forgiven. For example, Eldeen suffered the consequences of my affairs, and so did I. Eldeen's trust had been broken. Eldeen has been open about her unforgiveness and the bitterness that my behavior was causing her. Because she was so independent, she just dealt with things on her own, furthering our lack of intimacy. We see this so often in relationships. One person will hurt the other person and then apologize with a quick "I'm sorry. Now you need to forgive me." And then the offending party moves on their happy way, but in an affair, serious damage has been done.

Plus your mind never forgets anything. Never. The memories of the sinful behavior are still there, and the unfaithful spouse is always going to be able to bring those memories back to recall. Especially when something triggers the old responses. I get triggered by feeling condemned even today.

It goes back to self-condemning accusations of myself: I missed the mark, I sinned. The consequences of adultery are long-term consequences. You never forget the sin, and that makes you vulnerable to shame and guilt. So, in essence, shame and guilt are consequences that need to be dealt with.

The Enemy wants to bring up our past sins, throwing condemnation in our face. He knows the memories are still in our brain and he wants to use them against us. But when we surrender and seek God for forgiveness, the consequences are put on Christ. He overcomes the power of the consequences over us. It's not our willpower; we're choosing where we focus, giving up our will to Christ. So although we live with the consequences of our sin with memories for the rest of our life, we don't have any of the condemnation. In Christ's forgiveness, you are free of the burden. That's the difference.

Sadly, most people want to be free from even thinking or feeling anything after an affair. But people don't just get over the wound of betrayal. They don't instantly become transparent and open. I've counseled men who don't want to talk about their past mistakes anymore. For sure they don't talk about the consequences, but like it or not, destructive consequences are there, and they won't go away on their own.

*As I help couples through the reconciliation process, they must understand that respect must be earned while trust can only be granted.*

## Restoring Respect and Trust

If you have been the victim of betrayal, two things have occurred: You have been disrespected by the act, and your trust has been broken. As I help couples through the reconciliation process, they must understand that respect must be earned while trust can only be granted.

Respect is earned over time as the betrayer responds appropriately to God and his or her spouse. Now trust is a very different matter. It is something only the victim can grant to their betrayer.

### Eldeen

Shortly after Gene became a Christian, we had given our testimonies about what God had done in our lives to a church group. When we had finished, a man came up to me and asked, "Do you trust Gene now?" Truthfully, I said, "No. But I trust Christ in Gene." Where previously I had only God to trust, I could now trust God in Gene. Gene didn't hide or lie anymore, no longer afraid to tell me the truth. Our marriage became new and exciting and truly intimate.

We cannot wait for a person to be perfect enough for us to place our trust back in them. If we did, we would be waiting until eternity dawned. But we can trust a perfect God who is living and working in their heart.

With the perspective I have now, I tell women (or men),

who are struggling with overcoming the betrayal of their spouse, to focus on the truth in the midst of an incredibly dark time in their life, to focus on the light. This goes against the advice of the world, which says to focus on the darkness. Satan also wants us to obsess on what the darkness or the lie or the sin has done to us. If you want to move past the hurt, look for the Truth, the Light, in your spouse and focus on that. If Christ is in your spouse, you can trust Him to deal with them.

### Eldeen

Throughout the many years of our marriage, my trust of Christ in Gene has never wavered. In fact, my trust in God continues to grow. He is totally faithful and has enabled Gene to be faithful to me in our marriage for more than sixty years.

If the one betrayed does not grant trust to their spouse, there is no chance of experiencing true intimacy. For without trust, the relationship is based on nothing but performance. No one can be free to be themselves while their spouse "holds" their past sin over their head.

As a couple moves through the restoration process, there are a few things that must be done to reestablish respect and trust. First, the victim has a right to ask any question he or she wants to ask of the offender. I have them make a list of every question they would like to ask. Then I ask them why they need to know the answers. Will it cause you to be able to forgive? Will it bring you edification? Or will it end up destroying you? Once a victim finds out certain details, they cannot take the answers back. They will have to live with the knowledge and the mental images. Eldeen didn't want to know details. She didn't want to build an image about this person, that person, and condemnation toward them as well.

The issue is that the victim has the right to ask any question. Should the victim know all the answers? Only if it will be of benefit. The point here is that the attitude of the offender must be "You can ask me anything." Being open to any question helps regain trust. It says, "I am not going to lie to you. I am an open book."

> If the one betrayed does not grant trust to their spouse, there is no chance of experiencing true intimacy. For without trust, the relationship is based on nothing but performance. No one can be free to be themselves while their spouse "holds" their past sin over their head.

Second, there are boundaries that the offender must set up. If it is necessary, I will help a man end the relationship with a mistress by helping him write a letter or talking to her on the phone, whatever is needed to bring closure. These actions are a necessity to substantiate to the victim that the affair is over.

A self-imposed boundary one man set up is to call his wife at different times of the day, not because she asks for this but because he wants to remind her he loves her. I highly suggest that offenders have an accountability partner of the same sex. This will reassure their spouse that they are dealing with the truth.

Setting boundaries like these serves two purposes: 1) to protect the offender from entering into another adulterous situation, and 2) to reassure the victim that the affair is over and that their spouse is moving past it.

The response to betrayal that leads to true healing is found in turning to the mercy of God. It is when we come to the end of our own ability to cope with the pain of disloyalty—either our own inability to be loyal or someone else's betrayal of us—that we must turn to the *chesed* God.

The word *chesed* is used 240 times in the Old Testament, mostly to describe God and His faithfulness, loyalty, and mercy. *Chesed* comes from the verse: "The LORD is compassionate and gracious, slow to anger, abounding in love" (Psalm 103:8). He's the only One who is devoted to us, no matter what.

God's devotion exceeds our human understanding. It responds with love where we would expect hatred. In the book of Hosea, we are shown a glimpse of God's tremendous devotion to His people. Israel's unfaithfulness to the Lord is paralleled in Hosea's experience: His wife, Gomer, turned her back on her faithful husband to follow evil lovers. These are the words the Lord then spoke to Hosea: "Go, show your love to your wife again, though she is loved by another and is an adulteress. Love her as the LORD loves the Israelites, though they turn to other gods" (Hosea 3:1).

This is the loving-kindness and mercy God showed toward the Israelites who betrayed Him. This is the loving-kindness and mercy He shows each of us even when we are at our worst. God's devotion goes above and beyond a covenant commitment.

When we are hurt through betrayal, is it possible to apply this *chesed* love and mercy on a human level? What do we do with our anger so that it does not become bitterness, resentment, or revenge?

If someone hurts you, they deserve to be hurt in return. If someone has treated you unfairly, they deserve unfair treatment in return. That is justice. If you have been wronged, you want justice served. Now think of the many imperfect or unjust acts you have committed. Think of the people you have hurt, unintentionally or not. Are you as quick to claim justice? No, we plead mercy.

Mercy is defined as withholding from someone what he or she deserves as a result of his or her behavior. On the cross, we earned God's forgiveness. If Christ had not put on Himself what we justly deserve, we would be condemned, because no person can say they have acted perfectly toward everyone all the time. Since God has shown us mercy first, we are able to extend mercy to those who have hurt us.

In the book, *Tortured for Christ*, Sabina Wurmbrand tells of inviting a man into her home—the very man who had ordered the death of her parents in Romania. After she served him dinner, she told him who she was and that she knew he had her parents killed. She said, "I asked you to come because I want to extend you mercy and I want you to meet my Lord. He loves you." The man fell to the floor and wept. From a human standpoint, I can think of no greater example of *chesed* love and mercy.

I realize this scene may feel unrealistic for most hurting spouses. Sabina sounds like a saint. Most people couldn't do what she did. But I'm telling you that with the power of God living in and through you, you will be able to handle more than you ever thought possible.

*When we give our hurt and anger to God, He can help us turn it into mercy toward those who betrayed us. It is when we take the unrighteous acts of others to the cross and let the finished work of Christ deal with it that we find peace rather than bitterness.*

When we give our hurt and anger to God, He can help us turn it into mercy toward those who betrayed us. It is when we take the unrighteous acts of others to the cross and let the finished work of Christ deal with it that we find peace rather than bitterness. "For he himself is our peace, who has made the two groups one and has destroyed the barrier, the dividing wall of hostility" (Ephesians 2:14).

With all of my physique and strength, I could not stand up against the love of Christ. It is so powerful. This love in Eldeen enabled her not to leave me after my betrayal of her through adultery. I didn't know it at the time, but it was the love of Christ in her continuing to love me when I was unlovable. I knew full well that I did not deserve to be loved.

I hate to admit it now, but I tried to squelch that incredible love Eldeen showed me. If she would have hated me and left, it would have proved what I felt about myself—that I did not deserve her love, or any love for that matter. The love of Christ through Eldeen drew me to its Source.

When we experience God's love for us at our lowest of low points, we will gain a new understanding of love. Then we can learn to love others in a new way.

It is the devotion, the mercy, and the loyalty of God that enable us to overcome disloyalty and betrayal. This is true for the one betrayed and the betrayer. I was broken when I could not be loyal to Eldeen, try as I might. That is when I placed my trust in the *chesed* God through Christ.

If I hadn't surrendered to God, I most likely would have lost my family. Grief of my sin against God and my wife brought me to my knees. I couldn't change myself on my own. My inability to love led me to the Source of Love; my inability to be loyal led me to the Loyal One.

Christ put on Himself my imperfections and took the

penalty for my "missing the mark of perfection," or sin. This is mercy—I don't get what I justly deserve because Christ justifies me. I did not merit or earn it. When I think about Christ taking what I deserve and putting it on Himself so I might be justified, I am totally amazed. Why did He do it? Because He is *chesed* God—loving, slow to anger, showing mercy on those who do not deserve it.

Now if we believe this is true of God and that He is merciful toward us, how can we not show mercy toward those who wrong us or betray us, no matter how bad it hurts? Mercy cancels out justice. There is no need for justice since it is satisfied through Christ. That is how God looks at us if we accept His finished work on the cross. Then by faith, we can embrace that same power in extending mercy and forgiveness toward others.

Experiencing God's mercy has given me peace and incredible freedom. I bring that same freedom to others when I extend His mercy to them. I guess you could say that God empowers me to be *chesed*, and He offers that same power to you too.

### Be a Friend

During one of my radio programs, Mark joined me in talking about affairs. Several years ago, Mark had an affair with someone he met through his work. After twelve years of marriage (and three children), he divorced his wife, Gloria, to be with this other woman. Within a couple of years, God got hold of him.

Mark became convicted about his sin of the affair and the divorce. So he left the other woman and sought reconciliation with Gloria. She had walked with God through this painful time and was able to forgive Mark. They are now remarried.

When Mark thinks of the pain he caused his family, he is brought to tears. He empathetically urges men *not* to get into affairs. He says, "It is just not worth it. You lose your children; you lose your faith. It is tough to recover." Mark is so thankful to God and his wife for taking him back.

During our radio conversation, a gentleman called in. He suspected that one of his friends, whose marriage was bad, might be having an affair. He wanted to know how he should approach his friend.

Mark responded to the caller with some of his own experiences. "As I was going through this adulterous situation in my own life, I met with over eighty-two people from my church. I had all types of approaches from the fire and brimstone 'You are going to hell' to 'I love you brother, whatever is best for you.' Most of the approaches were very loving; they just wanted me to make sure I was doing the right thing. I did not care which angle they came from. I would not listen to anybody.

"What I have learned is to hit men head on, but with love. Give them a safe place to talk, respecting their privacy. You have got to listen and not be shocked by what you hear. Now when I talk to men who are struggling, I come right out and ask them, 'Is there someone else in your life?' Most of the time, there is."

Men, do you want to help your brothers in Christ? Then get involved in their lives. Are they about to derail their marriages? Do not just sit back and watch it happen. Loving your brother does not mean you condone his behavior. When they know you have their interest in mind, you can speak the truth in love.

We are responsible to share the truth in love. What the other person does with the truth is their responsibility. We have no control over it. As a counselor, I tell people that I am responsible to lead people to the truth; I am not responsible for what they do with it.

Whether you have been betrayed or are the betrayer, you have a choice. You can try to heal your pain your own way or give your pain to God. I can honestly say that when we allow God to heal our pain His way, He brings us through to a place we could never have engineered or imagined. God is the One who gives us hope in the midst of pain. In time, the wound of betrayal can be turned into good by God's grace. He can take you to a place of intimacy, deeper and more satisfying than you have ever known.

> *As a counselor, I tell people that I am responsible to lead people to the truth; I am not responsible for what they do with it.*

CHAPTER 12

# When Everything Possible Doesn't Work

M Y HOPE and prayer for every couple who comes to me for counseling is that they would submit themselves to God, work through their image problems, commit themselves to each other, and grow in experiencing intimacy the way God intended. Unfortunately, it does not always work out that way.

Deborah had been married for nearly two decades. She never wanted to get divorced or even imagined it could happen. After all, she and her husband were faithful Christians, actively involved in church and ministry. Until one day when Deborah learned the truth about her husband. He had deceived her repeatedly, indulging in unfaithfulness. Deborah's hopes and dreams of a godly, intimate marriage came crashing down around her.

Eventually, their marriage ended, leaving Deborah in overwhelming pain. She sat in my office, broken and weeping. "I will never get married again," she cried. "I do not even want to talk to a man. Maybe intimacy in the right sense was never meant to happen for me."

I hear words like Deborah's often. "I will just live alone. Intimate relationships are just not worth this pain and hassle." The pain of a failed relationship oftentimes overrides the desire for intimacy. Yet most of the people who have uttered those words will try again.

Three years after her heartbreaking divorce, Deborah remarried. She is beginning to experience, for the first time, true intimacy.

By no means in sharing Deborah's story am I saying we must get divorced and then remarried to find true intimacy. My point is even though people feel there is no hope in ever experiencing intimacy or connecting with someone on a deep, soul level, it can happen.

Many couples I have worked with were able to reconcile and grow closer and more intimate after betrayal; however, that doesn't always happen. It did not happen for Stephanie.

Stephanie was so fearful when she came to see me, alone. She was trying to grab hold of something to control, to heal, to whatever … anything to save her relationship. I told her we would do everything we could for God to save her marriage. We would attempt to deal with the problems and the betrayal; we would do everything possible through God's strength.

My first goal in marriage counseling is attempting to move couples beyond the blame game and fault finding.

Individually, each spouse must take responsibility for themselves and their own issues rather than blaming the other. I tell my clients, "You're responsible for your own actions, no matter what other people do. What goes on inside of you, as well as your response, is your responsibility." There is no room for blame in intimacy. At this point each spouse should be open to be vulnerable, to take a risk and deal with their fears. In Stephanie's case, that did not happen. Her husband refused to stop playing the blame game. Everything was Stephanie's fault. Yet he was the one living a double life. His accusations and manipulation seemed to escalate, instead of improving. Stephanie kept trying to do the right things, but the relationship continued to decline.

When a marriage relationship reaches this point, I've learned it's time to do less marriage therapy. In fact, if we continued, we would probably do more harm than good. When I do not see movement away from the blaming, the condemnation, or rejection, I often suggest individual counseling for a while, with periodic joint sessions. Something has to change before the negativism does more damage.

While the priority was still reconciling Stephanie's marriage, the situation necessitated a shift in focus. We backed off from joint sessions and focused on Stephanie and her issues as a person. While Stephanie wanted to continue in the counseling process, her husband wanted nothing to do with it.

## Going It Alone

Things were not changing in the marriage, but Stephanie could not stay this way. She couldn't stay status quo. Stephanie had been growing, and she wanted to continue to discover more of who she was and who God made her, but her husband would have none of it. By this time, she was fighting to save something that was one-sided.

I told Stephanie that if we trust God to meet her needs His way, she would come out of this all right, one way or another. We began to focus on what God was teaching her about herself. She had begun to see that maybe the image she had of herself as a person and as a woman were distorted. We began to deal with who she is, where she was right then, and discover more of the image God made her in. We focused on her fears and insecurities, not on changing her conditions or environment. We were not pursuing divorce, but reconciliation.

It did not take long for some of Stephanie's fears to surface. "I was afraid of being by myself and of not being able to take care of myself. I had gotten married when I was young and had really not been out on my own. I just could not take care of myself. On top of that, I didn't know who I was and who God made me. I had this image of who I felt I needed to be."

Not a bit uncommon, Stephanie felt that she was more of an extension of her husband than an individual person. She had always sought the approval of others and looked for someone to attach herself to. Her security became trying to be who somebody else wanted her to be—in this case, her husband.

"Growing up, I wanted to be the perfect child. Then I wanted to be the perfect wife and finally the perfect mother. But when it came to having the perfect marriage, it was not working because I could not control the other side." Stephanie was facing the reality that there could be a huge failure, that her perfect "hoped for" would come tumbling apart.

Here was Stephanie's dilemma: She believed that divorce is not necessarily what God intends. But she was in a situation where there was no reconciliation in sight. She was left alone to deal with the marriage herself.

When her crutches of acceptance were removed by her husband's rejection, she found she had lost her identity as a woman. Years of being blamed for the problems in their marriage squashed her femininity. "If you were only more of a woman …" She assumed there must be something wrong with her.

When she was young, Stephanie's personality was more of a compliant child. She tried to do everything just right so she would be more acceptable, more loved. She did her best to please, not wanting to disappoint anyone. If someone was disappointed, she took it that she was the one in the wrong. She'd apologize for things that weren't even her fault. "I am sorry" became the most used phrase in her vocabulary. She felt guilty for everything.

Unfortunately, Stephanie's desire and compulsion to please others could be, and often were, used to manipulate her. Stephanie grew used to being treated this way. As a result, Stephanie allowed her husband to manipulate her through guilt.

Stephanie had developed mechanisms of pleasing others to get acceptance. She was so compliant that she believed everything was her fault. As an adult she was stuck in the image of the perfect little child, always trying to please. Her husband was telling her the marriage problems were her fault. The message she received from him was: If she would just straighten up, if she would get her life together, the marriage would work. It seemed she could never fulfill the expectations that she believed had been placed on her. But like a hazy mirage, the closer she got to living up to the expectation, it would shift and change into another unrealistic demand. Stephanie accepted responsibility for things that were never her responsibility to begin with.

So often the roles we play—whether healthy or not—in our families of origin get twisted around when we try to reprise them in our marriages. For example, Stephanie's desire to please and to take the blame fit right into her husband's role of taking and blaming. These roles often serve as obstacles that keep people from being the person God created them to be.

For someone with Stephanie's makeup, it is usually very difficult to focus on his or her own issues. Those who are trying to be perfect, to please, do not want to look at the imperfect parts of their lives. (And we know that all of us are imperfect in our flesh.)

I encouraged and challenged Stephanie to catch those thoughts because they just may be lies. In order to change the way she thought about herself, she must take the thoughts and line them up against the truth. The truth will set her free, not beat her up or enslave her.

## Free to Be Yourself

Remember that I define intimacy as free to be yourself. Now, if you feel that to be loved you must be what somebody else wants you to be, you are not free to be yourself because you are not being yourself. But then who are you?

"What if I stop being what someone else wants and start looking inside me and find that I am not anything?" Stephanie expressed a very real fear. *What if I give up my mechanisms to get love and find that I am nothing?* Oh, but God does not make nothing. We are all created in God's image, with value, dignity, and purpose. Each one of us is one of a kind, absolutely unique and highly valued.

We went through quite a few sessions dealing with Stephanie discovering who God says she is versus the image she had developed that was not true. Her personality, the events in her life, and her reactions to them shaped her opinion of how she should react to life and others. She had been dealing with conditioning, not Creation (according to God's plan).

Little by little in this process, Stephanie's confidence in God and in herself increased. She began to be more confident in distinguishing what was and was not true about herself. When she took her focus off of others (in order to know how to please them) and set her gaze onto herself and on God, she made discoveries into who she really is.

Stephanie literally blossomed during this process. Still, she carried a heavy heart. She still wanted to restore her marriage.

Now that Stephanie was more confident in herself, we were ready to try to work on the marriage again. But we ran into the same scenario as before. Her husband could only blame Stephanie. This time, however, Stephanie had a healthy perspective of herself and was able to handle the accusations differently. She knew the problems in their marriage were not her fault. She also knew she could trust God for her future, whatever that may be.

When we started the counseling process, Stephanie struggled with God on where she was going. During her quiet times with the Lord in prayer, she felt like she was seeing His back all the time. One day, she told God she didn't feel like the intimacy with Him was there. Suddenly it was as if He said, "Do not look at my back but at where I am going. I am looking in a different direction. Just trust Me." That was a definite turning point for Stephanie.

Once Stephanie was able to recognize the truth, she saw the lie very clearly. For years, Stephanie's husband had been living a double life, although he constantly denied it all. She could no longer ignore his behavior and accept his accusations that it was all her fault. She could not participate in his lie and be the person God created her to be. Stephanie was up against a wall and needed to make a decision. This was the hardest decision she would ever have to make.

We looked at her alternatives. She could stay in the marriage if she was confident that is where God wanted her to be and if she were not submitting to a lie. But in her marriage, the lie that she was responsible for everything wrong kept slapping her in the face. By staying in the marriage, she was submitting to the lie, while her husband continued to live an unrepentant double life, which only caused her to lose self-respect.

Many times, Stephanie asked me what she should do. I told her I would be there for her, but I could not make the decision for her; she would have to decide. This was a new place for her to be. She had always found it easier to let others make her decisions because then she would not have to take the responsibility. But she had grown so much that she could take a stand on truth.

Still hoping and praying that it would bring about a change in her husband, Stephanie filed for divorce. Stephanie and her husband had been separated for a year before she filed. During the entire separation, her husband made no effort whatsoever to change. The condemnation and manipulation only continued.

As Stephanie looks back, she says, "God was my refuge. I could take my fears to Him. He was my strength through the whole thing. Where I once would have run back to the marriage for approval, I could now turn it over to God and stand on the truth." That was the key to the whole situation for Stephanie: She was confident of the truth. There was no doubt or guilt. Stephanie knew she had done all that God wanted her to do.

In some situations, the betrayed spouse will feel led by God to stay in the marriage. Eldeen stayed in our marriage, continuing to love me with Christ's love. I eventually responded to the love of God demonstrated through her faithfulness. But there are other instances where a person should not pursue their disloyal spouse.

Many women wrongly define biblical submission to their husbands as submitting to a lie in their marriage. They believe not seeking divorce is the higher ground. I have known Christian women to participate in pornography with their husbands in order to save their marriages. That is a lie. God never asks a woman to submit to a lie to bring about a truth.

When confronted with a divorce, some spouses finally face the truth and seek restoration. As I have said before, however, we do not live in a perfect world, and things do not always turn out perfectly. Reconciliation and healing in troubled marriages can only occur when both individuals are willing to participate in the truth. But some, in further rejecting the truth, actually run deeper into the lie. This is what Stephanie's husband did. He tried to pin the lie on her, blaming her for filing the divorce when it was his lifestyle that brought it about.

We often look at divorce as a sin. But when someone is controlled by sin, it will harden his or her heart. It is the sin itself that brings about divorce.

## Grieving Through Divorce

Throughout the separation and even when she filed for divorce, Stephanie had a glimmer of hope that her husband would turn around. But when the divorce papers were signed, the hope was gone. A sense of loss flooded over her.

Her marriage over, Stephanie was anything but happy. Divorce is death. Death to a dream. Death to what could have been. Divorce is often somewhat worse than a death because those involved must deal with a living corpse. No matter the circumstances, divorce is devastating and will have consequences. As any loss must be, divorce must be grieved.

Stephanie now had to deal with life alone. In the same way she overcame the pain throughout her marriage, she needed to heal from the pain of the divorce. Stephanie had to let God heal her wounds His way.

As with any hurt, the anger that results from divorce can turn to bitterness, resentment, and revenge. Stephanie was very careful to guard against it. I told her that in her pain, she could feel angry; that was natural. But she should not let the anger control her. She should give it over to God.

Then we talked about another tendency some people fall into after divorce—isolation. Immediately, Stephanie said, "I will never get married again! Why would I need a man?"

While this was a normal thought, I cautioned Stephanie not to think this way. This was her pain speaking, and it could close her off from a future relationship—one in which she could experience genuine intimacy. In the loneliness and the fear, it's difficult to believe that at times.

In order to give her heart time to heal (and not get into a relationship for the wrong reason), I suggested she not date for a significant period of time. As I had told her many times through the counseling process, if she would let God deal with the truth in her life as she sought to follow Him, God would meet her needs His way.

### A New Intimacy

About a year after the divorce, Stephanie met Greg. They began dating, and as their relationship grew more serious, they came to me for pre-marital counseling. I wanted them to fully understand the issues that could arise in their relationship. Before they married, they needed to do all God wanted them to do so that they would have absolutely no doubts. They did not need to live with any "should or should not haves" about their relationship. I told them to discern the truth and follow it, regardless of their feelings.

When we start getting close to someone, we have to decide if we are willing to take risks. The risk comes in opening ourselves up and becoming vulnerable. And that is a scary place. But to love is to risk being hurt. Whatever comes, we must leave it in His hands.

Once again, Stephanie had to face her fear. I did not want her to project her fear from her previous marriage into this new relationship. If she stopped here, as many have, she might miss out on what God had for her.

Stephanie and Greg were married after dating for one and a half years. Before long, Stephanie gave birth to their little boy.

To be sure, divorce is a last resort that we want to avoid if at all possible. At the same time, a healthy, intimate marriage requires two spouses who are willing to submit themselves to God and His work in their lives. When one of the spouses refuses to submit, God may be opening the exit door. At the same time, a new marriage of authentic intimacy after divorce is not a guarantee. Yet we can always trust God and His promise that He wants what is best for us. We can trust Him to meet our deep need for intimacy, one way or another.

In the midst of counseling, during her divorce, in the grieving process, and in her new marriage with Greg, Stephanie found that she could trust God. You can too. Whatever situation you are in, He will meet your needs if you let Him do it His way.

CHAPTER 13

# Freedom in Forgiveness

WE'VE TALKED a lot about unresolved pain throughout the previous chapters. That's because the truth rings true: If pain isn't dealt with, it will cause problems in your ability to share authentic intimacy with your spouse.

Every day, people walk into my office with an armload of hurts. Someone has done them wrong. We live in a world where we all miss the mark of perfection. Problems and difficulties arise when we bump into each other's imperfections. So how can we move on and release the pain? The key is forgiveness.

When I came to Christ, the full impact of my sin hit me like a sledgehammer. Wallowing in my sin, the thoughts "If only I had …" or "I should have …" threatened to cripple me. For missing the mark, I had to ask God for forgiveness. For violating Eldeen's trust and respect, I had to ask her forgiveness. For it all, I had to forgive myself. Forgiveness is canceling a debt that somebody owes. And sometimes that somebody is you.

Before we confront an issue where somebody has wronged us, we need to examine our own heart and see where we have missed the mark. None of us have the luxury of turning back the clock. There are no "do-overs." Many times, when someone is the betrayer or offender, they feel they have to make up for what they have done wrong, even after they have sought forgiveness from God and the one they offended. There is no way any of us can make up for what we have done wrong. In reality, we need to first confess our wrongdoings to God, then forgive ourselves, canceling our own debt we feel that we owe.

> Before we confront an issue where somebody has wronged us, we need to examine our own heart and see where we have missed the mark.

If we have sinned, we need to take it to the cross and accept God's forgiveness. It is Christ's work on the cross that paid the price for our forgiveness. By faith, when we ask for forgiveness, we are just appropriating that forgiveness, making it our own. In actuality, He has forgiven us even before we ask for it. Two thousand years ago, our "debt was canceled, paid in full" all because of Christ's sacrifice.

One of my clients struggled a long time with forgiving herself, overwhelmed with the weight of her sins. She kept looking for intimacy in the arms of men, but she didn't experience true intimacy until she received Christ's forgiveness and then forgave herself.

A young, single woman, Rebecca found herself pregnant and alone. The shame of having sex outside of marriage and the shame of becoming pregnant led her to the safest place in her perception—to an abortion counselor. She was told, "No problem, you will just have this procedure, and here are some pills so it will not happen again." Rebecca returned to her life, and everything was normal. But that was the deception. Her soul knew instinctively that something horrible had occurred, but she couldn't tell anyone because of the guilt she carried. The secret turned inward, and Satan used the lie that Rebecca was such a horrible person no one could love her, most certainly not God.

In despair, Rebecca told herself every day that God could never forgive her for ending a life He had started. Even though she committed her life to Christ, the lies were going through her subconscious like a tape recording. To Rebecca, she felt safer in the arms of a man who wanted her for sex than in the arms of God. Her fear of intimacy with God prevented her from experiencing any true intimacy at all.

Rebecca knew she needed to see a Christian counselor and address the shame, the guilt, and the despair. At the end of her rope, she feared her soul was going to die. That's when Rebecca came to see me.

Gradually I helped Rebecca through the forgiveness and healing process. With time, God broke her bondage to the lies she told herself. She learned to receive Christ's forgiveness, and gradually she came to the place of being able to forgive herself. This time she chose to not abort the baby, and gave birth to a healthy boy.

Rebecca will agree that next to her son, forgiveness is the greatest miracle in her life. As she told me, "I feel so free! I feel free to let that hurting young woman out from the bondage of the lies. I feel free to like myself and accept myself. If Christ can love me, I am truly loved. That is the truth that God offers us in Christ. And I can raise my son to know that same love."

In His time, God brought a wonderful man into Rebecca's life who loves her, past and all, especially her son whom he ended up adopting. After going through pre-marital counseling with me, they were married and continue to walk in forgiveness as a new family.

If you find yourself struggling to forgive yourself for any sin you have committed, know there is hope in the forgiveness of God. Through His grace and mercy, you can forgive yourself too.

## Forgiving Others

When we look at our own heart first, we can be sure we are not trying to correct another's behavior just so we will feel better about what we have done. It is then that we can take their sin (where they have missed the mark) to Christ. When we give their sin to Christ, we are claiming that their sin is "paid in full." We have canceled their debt to us. We can only do this when we place our trust in God to deal with the other person. We are taking ourselves out of the picture. What God does with the offender is up to Him.

Often, we find it difficult to forgive because we think when we do, we are letting that person get away with hurting us. So the thinking is, if we hang on to our hurt, we are going to punish them. That is the deception, because we are only punishing ourselves. We continue to be the victim. But the whole picture turns around when we apply God's forgiveness to ourselves and then to the one who has wronged us. Christ's finished work on the cross broke the power of our sin and the sin of others over us.

It is often not until someone is in the counseling process that they realize the emotional damage done by an adult in their past. Most often it is one of the victim's parents, sometimes both. Sometimes the adult abuser was another family member or member of the community. Understandably, as these memories and realizations surface, the adult who was a child victim feels hurt and angry. In order to heal and move past the pain, these adults must face their feelings and get to the point of forgiving their abuser.

I'm not saying the victim should dwell on their pain. Quite the opposite. It is important to identify the pain so the victim can find its source, enter into forgiveness, and then move on, giving the wounds space to heal. True forgiveness can only be offered through the power of Jesus, as Eldeen will be quick to remind you.

### Eldeen

When I choose to forgive my offender through Christ, I begin to realize that it isn't really me doing the forgiving—it is Christ forgiving through me. On my own, I don't have the strength or the ability to let go of the hurt. But when I bring my pain to Him, His grace begins to flow through my heart, giving me the strength to do what I could never do alone.

Jesus taught us to pray in Luke 11:4, "Forgive us our sins, as we forgive those who sin against us" (NLT). Those words hold a deep truth. When I choose to live them out, an unknown freedom begins to stretch across my heart—reaching me and then extending through me to those who have caused me pain.

I personally experienced this unexpected grace, and it freed me to love and forgive Gene. What once felt impossible suddenly became possible, not because I willed it, but because Christ worked that forgiveness through me. His love softened what was hardened, and His peace filled the places that once ached with resentment.

Some people in the healing process will choose to confront their abuser. This is the opportunity for the one violated to take back the respect that individual stole from them. I encourage victims of child abuse, with sought-out counsel and prayer, to say something like this to their abuser: "You sinned against me and that was wrong. I am not here to condemn you. I am simply telling you that it was wrong. I never told you that because I was too young at the time."

When you are at the point of going to your abuser and taking back your respect, your goal is not to get them to ask for your forgiveness. It would be wonderful if they did. In essence, you are there to release them from the bondage their sin had over you. Regaining your respect has nothing to do with their response to you.

What if the abuser is no longer living? Write them a letter as if they were. It is really not important whether they are alive or dead. It is not whether they respond in the right way or not. The issue is that you are able to confront the sin done against you and be released from it. That reestablishes your respect.

None of us can change our past, but at the same time, we can't deny it happened. As children, we were not responsible for what happened to us. Children are not responsible for what adults do. Instead of staying a prisoner to our past, we have a choice as adults. We have to recognize the effects of our childhood pain and grieve over our loss. As adults, we can look back and acknowledge how the past has affected us and then choose to move forward in maturity, not letting those past influences control us anymore.

Many victims, in fear of facing their pain, hang on to their loss instead of releasing it. They do not let God replace what they lost as a child. In essence, they continue to protect the loss rather than give it up and let God build something new. They remain victims.

After grieving, we must forgive our parents or those who caused our pain and hurt. In the process of granting forgiveness, we move into a new arena of being able to deal with life more effectively.

At this point, I need to point out the obvious. Even in a non-abusive relationship, people hurt each other. That includes marriage partners. Simply by being human, we betray and wound one another. We react out of impatience or selfishness or any number of causes, and our spouse is hurt enough to require confrontation and forgiveness. It happens all the time. No matter the origin of our pain, God is in the business of healing. On the cross, Christ broke the bondage of our sin and the results of someone's sin over us. Forgiveness allows us to experience the freedom.

## Forgive and Uh, What Was That Again?

Often, I am asked, "Does forgiveness mean I forget?" This notion possibly stems from the belief that God forgives and forgets, taken from Isaiah 43:25: "I, even I, am he who blots out your transgressions, for my own sake, and remembers your sins no more."

But I do not believe that God "forgets" as we might think.

> The LORD is compassionate and gracious,
> slow to anger, abounding in love.
> He will not always accuse,

nor will he harbor his anger forever;
he does not treat us as our sins deserve
or repay us according to our inequities.
For as high as the heavens are above the earth,
so great is his love for those who fear him;
as far as the east is from the west,
so far has he removed our transgressions
from us. (Psalm 103:8–12)

When we ask God to forgive us our sins, He removes the condemnation that should result. He chooses not to hold our sin against us. We could more accurately say that He chooses to remember our sins no more. God still knows all things. He always knows everything we have done, but He sees us as if we had never sinned.

Now, if you or I did not remember something, we would say that we had forgotten it. Everyone knows the feeling of wracking our brain for that bit of information we used to know: a person's name, a phone number, or where we parked the car. We may be convinced that the information is gone forever, but scientists say that our brains never lose anything (except in cases of injury). While we cannot recall everything that has ever happened to us, it is still there somewhere in our brain cells.

So does forgiving someone mean we forget? Not at all. But I do believe that the One who made our brain is capable of renewing our mind, causing it to dwell on things that are good and pure (Philippians 4:8). After we have forgiven someone, we need to concentrate on what is pure and right and just. This involves an act of our will and faith.

Forgiving someone who hurt us is never easy, but forgiving someone who has abused us, especially when we were a child, can seem nearly impossible. Yet it is a critical and necessary step in your journey to intimacy.

## Reconciling and Reconciling and ...

As I have previously mentioned, we can forgive others because Christ has first forgiven us. We also covered how forgiveness means canceling a debt that is owed. Once we grant forgiveness, we have released the other person from their debt to us. I will say this—once we have forgiven someone, we cannot take it back. Forgiveness is once and for all.

*Many people mistake forgiveness for reconciliation. Just because we forgive someone does not mean that everything has been reconciled in the relationship.*

Now reconciliation is a totally different matter. Many people mistake forgiveness for reconciliation. Just because we forgive someone does not mean that everything has been reconciled in the relationship. That is something we need to keep working on. Reconciliation is an ongoing process and not possible with everyone. Some victims of childhood sexual abuse, for example, can't go back to their abuser for reconciliation. Other victims of abusive relationships can't seek reconciliation because the offender is not safe or repentant. But for a couple to have relational intimacy in their marriage, reconciliation needs to happen alongside forgiveness.

I know all too well how we can quickly get back into the blame game and start pointing fingers at each other. Due to my own inadequacy, I am more sensitive to accusations, real or not. Each time Eldeen and I work through our disagreements and hurts, we are reconciling with each other. Restoring intimacy requires us to be completely honest and open, admitting our faults and weaknesses.

During the reconciliation process, we must confront the truth. When it comes to healthy confrontation, we should heed Scripture: " 'In your anger do not sin': Do not let the sun go down while you are still angry, and do not give the devil a foothold" (Ephesians 4:26–27).

Yes, all hurt turns to anger. It becomes sin if we allow that anger to control us, if we let it turn into bitterness, resentment, or revenge. We turn anger from sin when we work through our anger in a constructive way, confronting when necessary.

I believe in not letting anything between you and your spouse go by for very long. You need to deal with whatever has come between you. Define what the real issue is and work through it. It takes time and effort, but it is worth the restoration of the relationship.

## Setting Boundaries with Forgiveness

This being said, while we choose to focus on the good things, we proceed with caution and wisdom. Just because we forgive someone doesn't mean they will no longer hurt or betray us. That is out of our control, remember? It is advisable to be discerning where and when we renew our trust. Along with forgiveness, after experiencing a betrayal, we need to establish healthy boundaries in our lives.

A caller to my radio program stated, "I was betrayed and very hurt by someone. I went to this person as part of the healing. I have forgiven them but I am still hurting. How do I get over the hurt, even though I have forgiven the person?"

I do not believe the pain goes away quickly. It is a process. It is important to take the memory and pain of this person's sin—their betrayal of you—to Christ. Give it to Him, remembering that Christ died to break the power of this person's sin over you. Forgiving someone does not mean the memories and feelings will not come back. But every time they do, take them right to Christ.

Sometimes, our human nature wants to savor and hold on to the pain, remembering over and over and over again what the person did to us. But this destructive cycle will only beat us down. The memory and pain will come back. Instead of trying to deal with the pain yourself, give it to Christ and let Him handle it. Always remember that it is a process.

Forgiving someone does not mean putting yourself in a position to be vulnerable to that person again. We do not become a victim to show someone we love or trust them. If someone breaks into your home and steals from you, do you give them the keys to your house to show you have forgiven them? No way. Granting trust does not go hand-in-hand with your forgiveness. That would all depend upon how that person is responding to you.

I suggest setting a boundary of a little distance from the one who has betrayed you. This boundary must be made out of self-respect, not out of resentment or bitterness. Just exactly what the distance would look like and for how long, you would need to ask God. If God sees a purpose for you to try to reconcile with the person who abused you, that is one thing; if other people are telling you what to do, well, that is another. Sometimes people tell others what to do, but they are not the ones in pain.

Instead of questioning if you should let someone hurt you again, question if it would help him or her understand God's love. Is this really what God is calling you to do as an act of sacrificial love? If you are being used or manipulated, is it furthering the cause of God? Are you allowing yourself to be victimized because of fear of rejection or fear of not being loved or accepted? While the answers are difficult to discern many times, we must seek wisdom to know how to respond to those who have hurt us. But one step is certain: Forgiveness will open the doors in your heart for freedom, healing, and intimacy with your spouse. I understand the temptation to hold onto grudges, blaming those who have wounded us, but when you choose to forgive, your life has so many wonderful possibilities. This is what happened with Nikki.

Nikki and her husband fell hard for one another, and the first five years of their married life were wonderful. Both Nikki and her husband worked full time, reserving the rest of their time to be together. At the time, Nikki didn't realize she was trying to meet her needs by herself. Her job provided valuable approval for her work performance. She began focusing more time on her appearance to gain approval from others. Before long, she was looking for male approval in all of the wrong ways, meeting men at work and at happy hours. Soon her husband caught on. His wounds added to Nikki's shame. She began praying for a quick way out. Cancer? Car accident? Nikki's infidelity broke the intimacy she and her husband had once shared. His hurt from her adultery caused him to withdraw from Nikki. The neglect from her husband due to her unfaithfulness led Nikki down a deep depression that lasted for nearly ten years. Their marriage was in trouble, intimacy virtually non-existent.

When Nikki finally came to see me, we explored her past and discovered some valuable truth. We learned Nikki's dad wasn't ready to become a father. He bragged that his best years were in college. His drinking and partying were the stuff of legend. Tales exist of his fraternity brothers installing an actual alarm from a local fire station to wake him up for class. Handsome, funny, and the life of the party, he married a pretty co-ed, the sweetheart of the frat. After college, they married but their partying continued. Then Nikki was born.

Her mom was ready to settle down but her dad was not. This led to friction and more drinking. Nikki's dad stayed in a constant hungover rage. Eventually her parents got divorced, freeing her dad to remain in his element at bars, nightclubs, and strip clubs, where he often took Nikki, who was still a young child at the time.

Her dad's hedonistic lifestyle left Nikki with a distorted view of herself. She didn't understand the pure relationship that should exist between a daddy and his daughter, the safe protection of a loving father. Having been exposed to such a hyper-sexualized environment as a young girl, Nikki entered her teenage years looking for male approval in all of the wrong ways—sex, drugs, and alcohol—crippling her view of who she was as a woman. From her early teen years through college, Nikki traveled down a road of painful potholes of partying, promiscuity, and abortion. When she applied for work at a strip club and was offered the job, she was excited to tell her dad because he would be so proud of her. By the time Nikki met her husband, she had severe sexual shame.

Nikki's faith journey had started as a child when her mother was given a cancer diagnosis and found the Lord in the process. With the fear of losing her mother and troubled by the confusing sexual behavior of her dad, Nikki, even as a child, was desperate to believe in a Heavenly Father. But as she aged and became more immersed in her own sexual sin, she found it difficult to believe her Heavenly Father would meet her needs for love and approval. She tried to get her needs met in her old ways, but she admits her old ways were rotten. Although she longed to live a clean life, she kept reverting back to old patterns. Much like the people in Ephesians the apostle Paul warned about: "Having lost all sensitivity, they have given themselves over to sensuality so as to indulge in every kind of impurity" (Ephesians 4:19). Nikki could see her patterns of getting her needs met through male attention, but she didn't know how to break free. By the time they had four kids, Nikki's husband became completely disinterested in her. They shared very little intimacy, emotional or sexual, with each other. Much of Nikki's life was either facing or pushing down the pain.

That's when Nikki came to see me. I began to show her God's unconditional love—that she was God's unique masterpiece and she was loved by the One who hung the stars. Gradually, she did the painful soul surgery required to identify the lies and false beliefs she was believing about herself. She saw how the old patterns were born out of a distorted view of sex and a twisted view of herself. With time, she worked at abiding in the Word to learn new truths, "I am the vine; you are the branches. If you remain in me and I in you, you will bear much fruit; apart from me you can do nothing" (John 15:5). On note cards, she wrote the lies she'd been believing, and on the back of the cards, she wrote the truth of who she is in Christ. "I can't, but You can" became her mantra. Some flesh patterns quickly changed, and others were strongholds and required daily surrender (and still do). Finally she began walking through forgiveness for her father.

Then the worst possible thing happened. Her father's home was destroyed in a hurricane, causing him to move in with Nikki and her family. Nikki couldn't understand how the Lord would do this to her. The man she was trying so hard to forgive ended up on her couch, homeless and in very poor health. She couldn't imagine how she was supposed to care for this man who had taken her to strip clubs as a little girl.

When her dad had a heart attack and ended up in ICU, Nikki wrote an offense list while he was unconscious in the hospital and began praying for him, fasting, and seeking the Lord hourly. Her forgiveness journey took time as the Holy Spirit gently gave her compassion for the wounded little boy inside of her dad. He was hurting and so was she.

When her dad woke up, Nikki asked him, "Did you see Jesus?" Instead of answering her question, he angrily asked her to turn on the Cowboys game. But Nikki wouldn't let it go. Her Heavenly Father had given her a second chance, and she wanted her dad to have one too. So she did the hardest thing she had ever done—she became completely vulnerable with her dad. She confessed some of the negative things that had happened in consequence to his poor influence on her life. She described hurts done to her and wounds that she inflicted. She told him he was not the father she needed. Tears began to flow—from Nikki and her dad. Tears of confession, tears of responsibility, tears of forgiveness. God used that moment to bring a broken daughter and her broken father closer together.

Nikki's dad died a year later. The last thing she said to him was, "I love you so much." That would not have been the case without the Lord healing their relationship. And that healing extended into Nikki's marriage as well. As a result of the transformative changes in her life, Nikki was also able to be vulnerable with her husband and ask for his forgiveness. He also embarked on a deeper spiritual journey, humbly seeing where he was using coping mechanisms of overworking to avoid intimacy in their relationship. They each started growing in their individual intimacy with Jesus. With the sexual sins forgiven, they began to experience fresh intimacy in their marriage. Years later, they renewed their vows at their twenty-fifth anniversary. With extreme gratitude, Nikki's favorite thing to do is share with other women what the Lord has done in her life.

Forgiveness is freedom. Whether we are seeking forgiveness from God for our own sin or forgiving someone for his or her trespass against us, in every offense we have a choice. We can hang on to the hurt, refusing to forgive, opening the door to bitterness or resentment or revenge. Or we can forgive and experience a powerful freedom.

*Forgiveness is freedom. Whether we are seeking forgiveness from God for our own sin or forgiving someone for his or her trespass against us, in every offense we have a choice.*

# Part Four

The Quest Continues ...
Restoring and
Maintaining Intimacy

CHAPTER 14

# Live in Truth

WHEN PEOPLE come to me for counseling, they are usually motivated by pain. They want me to help fix the problem and stop the pain. Their feelings are real, and I don't tell them they are not to feel what they are feeling. At the same time, I cannot change their feelings. What I can do is help them change how they think about how they feel.

When we feel something, there is always an experience and a thought behind it. Our feelings may or may not reflect what is true. Remember, our senses are trained in this world. Whenever we talk about change, our feelings are the last to fall in line with the truth. But if we change the meaning associated with the experience and thought, then our feelings will come in line with the truth over time.

Change in any capacity involves risk. We are moving from the familiar to the unknown. And that can feel shaky. We don't know what's on the other side. Naturally, our feelings will fight change, even if that change is for our best. Our feelings do not know that. They just want to keep things status quo, even if that means denying the truth about necessary changes. My goal as a counselor is to keep exposing my clients to the truth. The truth will set you free, but it might not always be what you want to hear.

*The truth will set you free, but it might not always be what you want to hear.*

### Once a Weakness

The pain and betrayal I caused was a long time ago. It occurred in the early years of our marriage. In a sense, it seems a lifetime ago. But the realization of the pain I caused my wife is always before me. I do not want to downplay it. I do not want to forget it. Because I never want it to happen again.

Most Christians I talk to believe that the weaknesses in their flesh will go away. They think that since God has helped them overcome their sin once, they will not struggle with it anymore. That is wishful thinking. There is no truth to the belief that the weakness goes away completely.

Then how were we able to get past our sin in the first place? I have found there is an interesting thing that happens to us, especially new Christians. It happened to me. It is what I call a "grace bubble." After people come to Christ, oftentimes there seems to be a period of time when they are not having any problem with their particular weakness. This is only accomplished because of God's grace. Some people have told me that when they became a Christian, certain things they struggled with immediately disappeared and have never bothered them again. In some cases, they had battled physical addictions like smoking or drinking.

But when it comes to the sexual area, I do not believe the same is necessarily true. Sexual weakness usually does not automatically disappear, especially if someone has a pattern of getting their needs met—both physically and emotionally—outside of God's way. The door to vulnerability has already been opened.

I became vulnerable when I traveled for work in our early years of marriage. Looking back, I would say the temptation to "stray" was always there. I'd seen the pattern in my dad and uncle, and the temptation seemed to be passed on to me. But the opportunity did not present itself until the conditions were right: traveling, alone, drinking. While a Christian may experience a reprieve from their weakness, it inevitably shows itself again. Sometimes it does not take long, and sometimes it takes several years before that old weakness rears its ugly head. That is when we realize we have the same potential in our flesh to deceive or be deceived in the exact areas as we did before accepting Christ.

When the temptation hits, it is a shock. The temptation is so strong, and we feel so weak against it. "I thought I didn't have a problem with this anymore." Some people have thought that becoming a Christian or finding the right person would ease or stop the temptations. That is why some people change partners. Not true. Once a weakness ...

always a weakness. We need God's help to avoid repeating the sins of the past.

## Shame Contempt Cycle

It is important to remember that we each still have weaknesses in our flesh because of being born into a broken world, abuse we suffered, the sin we chose to commit—but we no longer have to be in bondage to it. Satan will bring up our past and try to beat us up with it if we allow him to do it. The Enemy will attempt to keep you a prisoner to your shame, which can lead to contempt. Shame is the feeling that you deserve to be rejected. Contempt is icy condemnation or hatred toward yourself, others, and God. For many of us, our past offenses make us prime candidates to feel perpetual shame and contempt about ourselves.

The shame-contempt cycle is a wicked trap that the Enemy uses to prevent you from being the person God created you to be. Intimacy with God, as well as with your spouse, has a hard time reaching you when you're stuck in the shame-contempt trap. Companions such as self-pity and hopelessness also loop around in that cycle. But, friend, you and I do not need to stay in that dead-end loop. God does not manipulate us through guilt to get us to stop sinning.

"Godly sorrow brings repentance that leads to salvation and leaves no regret, but worldly sorrow brings death" (2 Corinthians 7:10).

## Hope in Weakness

Thankfully, there is hope. The hope of breaking the shame-contempt cycle is the power of Christ. He can and will do it if you turn to Him, although the healing process is not a snap. It takes time and persistent work. Sometimes you might need the help of someone qualified and trained to help you walk through it. I assure you, there is a path to restoration and freedom. You can be the person God created you to be, free from the feelings of pain and condemnation.

The apostle Paul found hope and help in his weakness. He found that God's grace is more than sufficient.

> Three times I pleaded with the Lord to take
> [the thorn in my flesh] away from me. But he
> said to me, "My grace is sufficient for you, for
> my power is made perfect in weakness." There-
> fore, I will boast all the more gladly about my
> weaknesses, so that Christ's power may rest on me.
> That is why for Christ's sake, I delight in weak-
> nesses, in insults, in hardships, in persecutions,
> in difficulties. For when I am weak, then I am
> strong. (2 Corinthians 12:8–10) [addition mine]

Like Paul, I have found strength in God's grace. His grace is available to you as well. He knows how much we need it.

I think I have come to understand why God does not just remove our weaknesses in the flesh when we become

Christians. If He instantly erased our weaknesses, we probably would become self-sufficient and not depend on Him as strongly. Therefore, because of our weak areas of flesh, we must be super dependent on Him to help us not fall back into our old sinful patterns. And that is when we find that His grace is sufficient for us. In His grace, we have the victory.

## Avoiding the Sins of the Past

On a practical level, we should all set up boundaries in our areas of weakness. Out of respect for yourself and your spouse, these boundaries are a protection. For example, if you have fallen sexually, you should use discretion in being alone with a member of the opposite sex. Professionally, I see women alone in the counseling room, but I will not see them alone outside of the office. The principle here is to never put yourself in a vulnerable position to act on a temptation. I tell men not to try to meet another woman's needs outside of their wife being involved in the process.

Another boundary that should be set up is establishing an accountability partner. In addition to being accountable to your spouse, a man should be accountable to another man, a woman to a woman. In this way, your spouse will be comforted in knowing that you are being honest about your weakness with another person who can understand and encourage you.

I have been asked, "Should husbands and wives share their attractions and temptations with each other?"

It depends on where these individuals are in their relationship. The important point here is accountability. I am not sure it is wise to go home and share every time you were tempted. After I accepted Christ, I wanted to be transparent with Eldeen and tell her about the struggles I was having without putting the burden on her. I meant well and wanted nothing to come between us. Later on, I learned that she really does not need to know everything I am struggling with, every single time I struggle with it. What she does need to know is that I am dealing appropriately with my struggles.

On the other hand, if you are afraid of sharing something with your spouse, something is wrong with your intimacy. Eldeen and I have an agreement between us that we do not have to tell each other every time we have a tempting thought. But if either of us is afraid to share it, we have a problem. When I do share something with Eldeen, I do not need to give her all the gory details. But warning bells go off in my mind if I am afraid to tell Eldeen the truth that I am struggling at all. The warning is that I am keeping secrets, and secrets prevent intimacy. They also open the door to sin.

I've had accountability partners through the years—people who can ask the tough questions of me and help me take my struggles to Christ. Eldeen can have confidence in me when she knows I am accountable to another man.

*If you are afraid of sharing something with your spouse, something is wrong with your intimacy... if either is afraid to share, we have a problem.*

At the same time, Eldeen and I hold a certain account-ability to each other as well. Although we may not share every detail with one another, we are committed to telling the truth. At times, that requires bringing up a concern.

Over the years there have been times when Eldeen has approached me with concerns, and we've been able to talk openly about the temptation I'd been experiencing. But the consequences, the reality of how my betrayal had hurt her, never fully go away. Eldeen asked me a direct question years after the infidelity. To be transparent, I answered honestly, only to be met with her honest response in return—a response that still reflected the hurt I'd caused her.

### Eldeen

In the past, when it came to confrontation, I held too many things in. Then after Gene became a Christian, the Lord gave me freedom to express my viewpoint, especially when it was different from Gene's. Of course, since I had not done that very often, I did not always do it properly. Even today, I have the quick ability to make statements very concise. My exhortations can be quite direct, without much cushioning.

During a discussion, Eldeen may come up with a "did you ever think of this … ?" kind of statement. Right then I have a choice. I can receive Eldeen's insight or exhortation as a gift from God or as a condemnation or rejection. It all depends on whether I take the inadequacy I feel at the statement to God or turn it back to Eldeen, telling her to change the way she talks to me. Of course, the latter choice won't foster much intimacy with my wife.

Recently, Eldeen confronted me on something that was true, and I didn't like it when I heard it. The more I thought about it, however, I realized she was right. I truly believe God has given Eldeen the gift of exhortation. Now ... when she uses that gift and tells me the truth, I may not like to hear it. Initially, my feelings of guilt may be tapped, and I could think Eldeen is trying to put me down rather than help me. In my mind, my "offending" words or actions are coming out of a heart and a life of loyalty and commitment. So how could she question my motive?

True confession: I am still reaping the effects of the Fall. In my distorted flesh, I will take Eldeen's helpful exhortation as a glaring spotlight on my inadequacy. If I do not take my feelings of inadequacy to Christ first, I will react to Eldeen in a hurtful, destructive way. I could even short circuit the help that God wants to provide—from the very one He has given me as an intimate helpmate.

In the same way, if Eldeen does not take her insecurities to Christ first, she will put unrealistic demands on me. To her credit, since early in our marriage before I was a Christian, Eldeen has always looked to God, not to me, for her security. She learned how to live in God's truth well before I did. Thankfully, God in His mercy accepted me in my brokenness, and He is helping both of us to live in His truth. We're no longer trapped in the false beliefs instilled during our childhoods. Eldeen is not my caretaker; she is my soulmate. I am not her conqueror; I am her partner.

So many disconnected spouses remain stuck in false beliefs from their past, continuing to suffer the damage those false beliefs have caused. If that's you, God is calling you to His truth. He will faithfully lead you on the journey to connecting in intimacy—with Him first. And then with your spouse, if he or she is willing to surrender to Christ and walk this path with you.

The journey will include retraining you on how you see yourself. What you think about yourself and how you respond in relationships is based largely on the image you formed as a child. We develop a picture of ourselves from our significant relationships—our parents, siblings, friends, teachers, coaches—our environment and the circumstances we experience. The image we form is distorted because it is not based on something totally pure and true. Fortunately, we do not have to continue to live in a lie.

"This means that anyone who belongs to Christ has become a new person. The old life is gone; a new life has begun!" (2 Corinthians 5:17, NLT).

When a person becomes a Christian, a process is set in motion. In an instant, the inner man is restored back to its original, perfect image. Not so with our flesh. The return of our outer man to a perfect state with our inner man takes time, a lifetime to be exact. This process is called sanctification, and it will not be complete until we meet the Creator face-to-face.

This sanctifying work of God in our lives is the retraining or renewing of our senses and of our minds. He is restoring the false image we have of ourselves.

"But solid food is for the mature, who by constant use have trained themselves to distinguish good from evil" (Hebrews 5:14).

This retraining involves breaking our dependency on anything or anyone we allow to meet our needs in the wrong way. Through Christ, we can discern the truth about ourselves and others. But there is one prerequisite you and I must meet. We need to give the control of our lives to God. We must allow God to meet our needs His way.

"You were taught, with regard to your former way of life, to put off your old self, which is being corrupted by its deceitful desires; to be made new in the attitude of your minds; and to put on the new self, created to be like God in true righteousness and holiness" (Ephesians 4:22–24).

God created you as a beautiful human being in your mother's womb, hardwired with your own uniqueness, remember? Then life got a hold of you and caused you to doubt, dislike, and distrust who God made you to be. God wants to show you how much He loves you and how special you—and your spouse—are. He wants you to see yourself through His loving eyes, no matter what your past whispers to you.

One word I like to use to describe this part of your journey is "renew." Isn't that a great word? God wants to renew how we view our lives, beyond what we sense is true in this fallen world. The way to renew our senses and our minds is to embrace God's truth. Not the world's "truth." Not the wounded "truth" from past trauma. His truth.

"Do not conform to the pattern of this world, but be transformed by the renewing of your mind. Then you will be able to test and approve what God's will is—his good, pleasing and perfect will" (Romans 12:2).

God longs for you to walk in intimate relationship with Him, and for your marriage to be a reflection of His intimate love. That can only happen through Him ... and that is the most spectacular truth of all.

## CHAPTER 15

# Restoring God's Design for Marriage

B EING ORDAINED, I have officiated at many weddings. In countless ceremonies, the couples have included well-known verses from the book of Ephesians. This section of Scripture gives instructions to husbands and wives, specifically about love and submission. I am sure each newlywed couple has every intention of following the admonition.

If you're not familiar, this Bible passage tells women to discover how to submit to their husbands through Christ and tells men to discover how to love their wives as Christ loved the church and as they love their own bodies. But I honestly believe that besides loving God first, there are no more difficult vows to keep day by day. In and of ourselves, we do not have the ability to live out this teaching in our relationships. Only Christ gives us the power to have that kind of selfless relationship in marriage.

In my counseling practice, the men I see are telling their

wives how to submit, and the women are telling their husbands how to love. Somewhere along the line, men and women feel they need to tell the other how they should go about fulfilling their role according to what the Bible says. This is far from being productive or beneficial.

I've seen these precious Bible verses used incorrectly, even abusively, too many times. Women feel oppressed. Men feel worthless, like they can never match up to what they're supposed to do as godly husbands. There has been a lot of fear and misunderstanding surrounding these instructions. Of course there has! The Enemy wants to mess with God's design for an intimate marriage, so he makes sure confusing messages get thrown around when it comes to submission and loving like Christ. We need to remember that God wants what is best for us, even when it's not easy. And He especially knows what is best for us in our marriage relationship. It was His design all along.

Let's take a look at Ephesians chapter 5:

> Wives, submit yourselves to your own husbands as you do to the Lord. For the husband is

*Women feel oppressed. Men feel worthless... The Enemy wants to mess with God's design for an intimate marriage, so he makes sure confusing messages get thrown around when it comes to submission and loving like Christ.*

the head of the wife as Christ is the head of the church, his body, of which he is the Savior. Now as the church submits to Christ, so also wives should submit to their husbands in everything.

Husbands, love your wives, just as Christ loved the church and gave himself up for her to make her holy, cleansing her by the washing with water through the word, and to present her to himself as a radiant church, without stain or wrinkle or any other blemish, but holy and blameless. In this same way, husbands ought to love their wives as their own bodies. He who loves his wife loves himself. After all, no one ever hated their own body, but they feed and care for their body, just as Christ does the church—for we are members of his body. "For this reason a man will leave his father and mother and be united to his wife, and the two will become one flesh." This is a profound mystery—but I am talking about Christ and the church. However, each one of you also must love his wife as he loves himself, and the wife must respect her husband. (Ephesians 5:22–33)

Tough orders, right? Perhaps. But when we surrender our human understanding to God's wisdom, He will open our eyes and our hearts to the greater meaning behind these instructions. Eldeen and I will take turns speaking: first to the women, and then I will speak from the man's perspective.

## Wives, Be Subject to Your Husbands

*Eldeen*

Within my family and the families of friends, I never saw wives submit to their husbands as to the Lord. It was never talked about. When I got married, submission was not a concept I thought about or even considered.

A few years into our marriage, I yielded my life to Christ. Without fully understanding what it all meant, I said "Yes" to His will for my life. And everything changed. I heard with new ears and saw with new eyes. When I read the Scriptures, I understood them. I started praying and told God that I would do anything He wanted me to do.

Immediately, He began speaking to me about my marriage. Before, I had been so focused on what Gene had done wrong; his adultery was no small thing. Now I saw my own sin. I was not very submissive and had developed a bitter attitude.

First, I had to learn to submit to the Lord. For two years before Gene accepted Christ, it was just me and the Lord. I had such an intimate relationship with God. He gave me the ability to hang in there and love Gene, even at his worst. It was like I had a direct line to God. His voice and leading was always so clear. But once Gene became a Christian, the whole picture changed. God would now speak to my husband and lead me through him. I wondered if it was possible for God to speak to his heart and help him lead us as a family. I now had to learn to submit to a person who makes mistakes. It is one thing to submit to a perfect, all-knowing God. But to submit to a fallible man? It was a big transition for me. But it was undeniable that Gene had changed; he truly was a new creature. I knew I needed to obey God and continue to trust Him now with a new man.

We women have a fear of submitting to someone we see make mistakes. We also have to submit to someone who thinks, feels, and processes things differently than we do. Everything would be great if our men would just listen to our intuitive feelings. You know what I mean. We can't explain why we know something about the kids, our home, the neighborhood, you name it. We just know. Yet even with our God-given sensitivities and intuition, we are to submit to our husbands. Why? Because as we submit to men that we see, we are learning that God is more powerful than us or them or our situation or circumstances.

I think in regard to submission, we women need to take a passage in I Peter to heart.

Wives, in the same way submit yourselves
to your own husbands so that, if any of them
do not believe the word, they may be won
over without words by the behavior of their
wives, when they see the purity and reverence
of your lives. Your beauty should not come
from outward adornment, such as elaborate
hairstyles and the wearing of gold jewelry or
fine clothes. Rather, it should be that of your
inner self, the unfading beauty of a gentle and
quiet spirit, which is of great worth in God's
sight. For this is the way the holy women of
the past who put their hope in God used to
adorn themselves. They submitted themselves
to their own husbands, like Sarah, who obeyed
Abraham and called him her lord. You are her
daughters if you do what is right and do not
give way to fear. (1 Peter 3:1–6)

The world places such a high value on the exterior
appearance. We can't get away from it—TV, billboards,
magazines, movies. Many of us have bought into it and
carry the notion into our marriages. We ask ourselves
while looking in the mirror, "Do I look sexy?" But do
we ask, "Do I look godly?" Women, the questions we
ask ourselves will determine the fruit in our marriages
and relationships. Will we reap short-lived excitement

or longevity and intimacy? Men, too, need to think different questions to encourage their wives to seek God's will.

When I read the passage from I Peter 3, I am impressed with the fact that our actions, in this case submission, must come from the state of our heart—a gentle and quiet spirit. I believe the only way any person can have a quiet spirit is if they are wholly dependent on and connected to God. Women, we honor God when we submit to and respect our husbands, but there is no other way to do that unless we first submit to the Lord. Knowing that God is in control of any situation gives us peace and assurance.

I must address what I call the dark side of submission. There are so many books out on submission, and I have read many of them. I am not saying I have cornered the market on understanding it, but I do see that submission is a subject that can be misunderstood and misused. Some women, by personality and/or upbringing, are very shy and quiet. This type of woman may believe that submission means never verbalizing to her husband what is on her heart. I would encourage this woman to ask God what He would have her do or say. God may just prompt her to do the opposite of what her flesh is trained to do ... and speak up.

Then there is the much more serious misuse and distortion of submission. I have heard stories of Christian women participating in blatant sin just because their husband asked them to. Do not submit and join in anything you know is contrary to God's Word. I cannot say this strongly enough: God would never want you to submit to a lie or a sin in submitting to your husband.

For those walking through the ache of a disconnected marriage, hope and faith may feel fragile—but they are not lost. I have been there. I watched the Lord intervene through many small and great miracles, and for a time, I believed that story would unfold the same way for everyone seeking truth, change, and healing rather than lies. That became a beautiful reality for Gene and me, but I learned it is not the outcome for every marriage.

For me, my greatest aha moment came when I realized my faith and hope were misplaced—I had been asking Jesus Christ to change Gene. When I surrendered that and placed my faith fully in Christ Himself, trusting Him to work first in me and to write whatever ending brought truth, peace, and redemption, my heart found rest. Even when circumstances don't change as we pray, Jesus remains faithful, present, and powerful to heal, guide, and restore what is most important—our hearts and our hope.

## Husbands, Love Your Wives

Okay, now it's my turn. We husbands are to love our wives as Christ loves the church. I did not learn to love correctly. Like most of you, I had imperfect examples. I had to learn to love through the power of God's Spirit. Still, I have not mastered it yet in my flesh (Eldeen will attest to that). If I ever get to the point I think I can love in my flesh as Christ loves the church, I am in trouble. That is why I need to place my faith in Christ.

I have got a question for you husbands. Think of this past week. Have you found it difficult to love your wife as Christ loved the church? In action, attitude, or thought? If you had difficulty, it was not the fault of your wife. It is easy to love your wife when she is sweet and cooperative. But the true measure of your love is tested when things are not going your way.

When you love your wife as Christ loved the church, you put yourself in a vulnerable position. That is a frightening prospect because, typically, men are afraid to give up control of their lives. This fact is evidenced in that, of the two in a marriage, women tend to come to Christ first. This was true in our marriage. I believe that until the day I die, I will be scared to give up control and put myself in a position to let go and love.

If you are in a difficult situation, Satan wants you to quit and throw in the towel. I come up against this every day with couples in conflict who just want to give up. They say, "It is not worth it!" But it is at this point in a marriage when I believe we truly learn what it means to love by faith. The battle is to keep going and continue loving each other by faith, even more so for the husband to love his wife the way he's supposed to. It is not easy. In fact, it is not even humanly possible.

Daily, I have to submit to Christ to love Eldeen in the way that He loves the church. I must cross over the fear of giving myself totally to her. I can only do this through the power of Christ. But when I do, I experience an indescribable freedom.

During our marriage, I have learned ways to show Eldeen that I love her. Men, I cannot stress this enough: Be a student of your wife. Learn what makes her feel loved and then do it. And do it frequently. One of the ways I communicate my love to Eldeen is in writing her poetry. She will be the subject of my sonnets for years to come.

Most of all, a wife needs her husband to be transparent, free to openly be himself with her. Again, that is the definition of intimacy. Our wives need us to share our feelings with them. While this doesn't seem a lot for the women to ask, we men tend to see it differently.

We men tend to hide or deny our feelings because we think they are unmanly. The redeemed man is set free to be motherly, to portray the tenderness of God. In his book *I Married You*, Walter Trobisch writes about his experience as a missionary in Africa. He found that the Kilga tribe in East Africa had a name for God: Bikiko, meaning "a god who carries everyone on his back." In this tribe, it was the responsibility of the mothers and older sisters to carry children on their backs. A father would never do this. So why would they attribute such distinctly feminine attributes to the God of the universe?

I can only surmise that they learned of God's words recorded in the book of Isaiah:

> Listen to me, you descendants of Jacob,
> all the remnant of the people of Israel,
> you whom I have upheld since your birth,
> and have carried since you were born.
> Even to your old age and gray hairs
> I am he, I am he who will sustain you.
> I have made you and I will carry you;
> I will sustain you and I will rescue you.
> (Isaiah 46:3–4)

God broke the mold for the Kilga men, indeed for all men. To portray Bikiko, one of their artists made a wooden carving of a man carrying two children. The child on his back had the face of an adult, and the weaker child was held in his arms. The carving is a symbol of a God who takes care of human beings with the tender care of a mother.

As men, we are often not in touch with our feelings because we think we must express everything objectively without any feeling. But this is a sign that our spiritual lives are poverty stricken. We cannot mirror or radiate the tenderness of God because we have not experienced it ourselves. God wants to be loved as a father and mother are loved by their children, as a man by his wife and a wife by her husband, as a friend by a friend, and as a caring nurse by a sick person. God finds great joy when we express our feelings toward Him.

Before a man can feel and express his feelings, he often has to go back to the past and deal with the hurting, frightened, hating child within himself. Do you remember the song "Jesus Loves the Little Children"? Well, Jesus loves the wounded children in our hearts. He is the only One—the same yesterday, today, and forever—who can walk into our past, to the time even before we were born, and place His healing and comforting hands on all those deeply sensitive spots we try to cover up with our armor of invulnerability.

The healing of memories enables a man to have the courage to be motherly and express his deepest longings and feelings. The redeemed man no longer needs to retreat into his fortress because his past hurts have been exposed to the light and healed. He is able to stand unguarded, emotionally naked and vulnerable, ready to risk being wounded again. His fear is gone.

Men, we will continue to strive against this tendency to hide our gentler side. Our culture perpetuates the notion that "real men don't cry." But God enables the redeemed man to share the deepest part of his soul—tears and all. And I can tell you (and Eldeen will vouch for me on this as well) that a redeemed man is a real man any day.

## Mutual Submission

On the subject of submission, we as Christians need to keep one thing in mind. You can't live out the truths of Ephesians 5 unless you live out submission to Christ. When you fully submit your life to Christ, He teaches you how to be intimate—first with Him and then with one another. I hear a lot of discussion around the topic of submission, and usually it centers on the wife needing to submit to the husband, period. But there is so much more to this beautiful concept.

We have been designed from the beginning to have an intimate relationship with our Creator, to submit to Him in all things, and from that secure place within us we are then free to love and submit to our spouse. That kind of mutual submission frees us from the legalism that paints a picture of a woman saying yes to her husband's every whim. A legalistic view of submission isn't what Ephesians 5 is referring to at all. The Bible says, "Submit to one another out of reverence for Christ" (Ephesians 5:21). Clearly, we are instructed to submit to one another as unto the Lord, because we love and honor Him.

Submitting your will first to Christ is the key to having a deep, intimate marriage. When husband and wife submit to Christ together, they are able to submit to one another the way God designed it, in mutual submission because of our love and surrender to Christ and His plan for us.

I recall a significant time when Eldeen and I had to work through the principle of mutual submission. I was considering making a transition in my work and had gone away to pray for a few days. God spoke to me intimately through Isaiah 50:4. As I read the Scripture, I felt God leading me to the importance of learning God's Word. The prophet Isaiah described what I was feeling so strongly: "The Sovereign LORD has given me a well-instructed tongue, to know the word that sustains the weary. He wakens me morning by morning, wakens my ear to listen like one being instructed." I just knew I was supposed to focus on being well instructed in the Bible.

I came home excited that God had answered my prayers and had given me peace and direction from His Word. The Scriptures God led me to did not tell me specifically the path to take, but I felt led to further my knowledge of God's Word by attending Bible college or seminary. As I shared all this with Eldeen, she affirmed me in the desire to grow in furthering my education, but she did not believe we should leave the city we were living in.

Rather than submitting to me and ignoring her own sensitivity to God, Eldeen shared her concerns with me. And rather than demanding that my wife bow in submission to my way of thinking, I took her concerns seriously. Together we prayed and sought the Lord for His will. It was out of this place of prayer and mutual submission that God united us, and we both experienced God calling and leading me into counseling, a ministry where God has blessed and helped hundreds of individuals and couples over the past four decades. This wouldn't have happened if I had insisted Eldeen submit to me.

Husbands and wives, God is calling us to be there for each other—in open, authentic intimacy. This is achieved when we first submit our lives to Christ and then to one another in mutual submission. And the great thing is … He shows us how and He helps us accomplish it. We can trust Him to lead us in His perfect way. There is intimate freedom in that truth! If there's one thing I've learned in my counseling practice and in my own marriage: God's design for marriage can be trusted.

CHAPTER 16

# Nurturing Intimacy
# for a Lifetime

T HE JOURNEY to intimacy is a constant one. In my experience, no couple ever reaches a point in their marriage
where they can say, "We have arrived!" Issues that pose a
hindrance to being intimate will continue to surface in every
marriage. Each of us has to work at staying connected.

Eldeen and I have come a long way in our marriage. We
have three grown children and now five grandchildren and
one great-grandchild. In some respects, things are easier. You
know the old saying, "A little bit older, a little bit wiser." I
believe in our case that is true. Eldeen and I have grown in
our knowledge of ourselves, each other, and the Lord.

Yet our knowledge of each other also still holds the potential for great hurt. Because of all that has happened in
the past, we both have sensitive areas that can be easily hurt
through careless words or neglect. In addition, we have an
Enemy who wants us to still throw in the towel after all

these years and give up when the times are hard or when we have been hurt.

That means we never stop working toward intimacy.

*Communication is the key to maintaining intimacy in a marriage. In this day and age, with so many things vying for our attention, communicating (sharing and listening) can be downright difficult.*

### Special Times Together

Communication is the key to maintaining intimacy in a marriage. In this day and age, with so many things vying for our attention, communicating (sharing and listening) can be downright difficult. I must confess, with everything swirling around us, I oftentimes have a hard time giving Eldeen my undivided, focused attention. Even when we are at home, it is a challenge for me to keep the mental "to-do list" from capturing my thoughts. Often Eldeen and I must spend time alone, away from everybody and everything. We have a favorite spot at a local lake, where we go to talk, pray, and plan.

For our twenty-fifth anniversary, we had the opportunity to go to Bermuda. What a blessing! I can't remember feeling so relaxed and refreshed as we enjoyed discovering new things together. We were inspired to remember and recapture the intimacy we had experienced previously in our marriage.

Together and focused, we were able to delve into each other's soul. Talk about discovery!

This type of focused time together is essential for every married couple. No matter if you go to an exotic locale or some other more local place, take time to be alone, away from the interference of daily life. It takes discipline to work this into your schedule. Squeeze as many of these special times in as you can. You will be rewarded as your love relationship continues to grow deeper and deeper.

So … how do you go on from here? To sum it up: Focus on what you have control of through Christ and let go of what you do not have control over. Determine to live through the righteousness of Christ instead of trying to correct the unrighteousness in your past (you cannot do it anyway). His righteousness covers our sin when we admit our wrongs and ask for His forgiveness from a contrite heart. Begin to see yourself as God sees you: as if you always had it right. Believe it. It is absolutely true.

Choose forgiveness—for yourself and for others—instead of staying stuck in bitterness or resentment. Place your trust in God to protect you as you open yourself in transparency and trust Him to show you when boundaries are necessary. Continue pursuing intimacy with Christ. Choose to live in His truth, retraining your senses and your mind to bring about God's will in your life. That includes authentic intimacy and deep connection with your spouse.

## Into the Sunset

"Let your wife be a fountain of blessing for you. Rejoice in the wife of your youth ... may you always be captivated by her love" (Proverbs 5:18–19, NLT).

I am a man truly blessed to still be absolutely captivated by the wife of my youth. I loved her as a young woman. I loved her as the mother of my children. I love her still as a grandmother and great-grandmother. What a pleasure it is to grow old with such an incredible woman! If it were not for God intervening in our lives, I would have missed it all.

Eldeen and I have worked through pain from our childhood and the hurt in our marriage, letting God fix it His way. With His help, we have found the path marked "To Intimacy." It is a journey we have become quite familiar with these many years. It is also a journey on which we have yet so much more to discover. It is a journey we will be on, joyfully, the rest of our lives. I would not want it any other way.

I hope and pray that you and your spouse will choose to continue on this same path to intimacy as well. With God's help, you can journey down the path of life together in open transparency, free to be yourself, knowing you are truly loved. That is intimacy the way God designed it.

*With God's help, you can journey down the path of life together in open transparency, free to be yourself, knowing you are truly loved. That is intimacy the way God designed it.*

# Once Upon a Time

*by Gene Schrader*

Once upon a time, I knew a girl who was cute
    as a button.
Once upon a time, I met a girl who was kind
    and considerate.
Once upon a time, I met a girl whom I walked
    four miles in a snowstorm to see.
Once upon a time, I met a girl whom I would
    talk to for hours on the phone from a
    phone booth in the middle of a Wiscon-
    sin winter.
Once upon a time, I met a girl whom I would
    write a letter a day to while apart.
Once upon a time, I met a girl whom I would
    ride a bus across town to see.
Once upon a time, I met a girl whom I would
    say to: "I love you more than anything."
Once upon a time, I married that girl.
Once upon a time, I knew a woman who bore
    our first child and our second.
Once upon a time, I knew a woman who did

not run away when difficult times came into our relationship.

Once upon a time, I knew a woman who endured betrayal, disease, and displacement in times and still did not run away.

Once upon a time, I knew a woman who loved me when she should have hated and despised me, and I could not understand why she did not.

Once upon a time, I knew a woman who gave and gave when she could and should have taken.

Once upon a time, I knew a woman who forgave me when I did not deserve it.

Once upon a time, I knew a woman who introduced me to the One who could forgive ... Jesus.

Once upon a time, I knew a woman who, after being betrayed, was asked, "Do you trust Gene now?" She stated, "No, but I trust Christ in him."

Once upon a time, I knew a woman who followed her husband in his present attempt to follow Christ.

Once upon a time, I knew a woman who still loves me when I know at times I am very unlovable.

Once upon a time, I knew a woman who
has become a grandmother and whom
I cherish watching the moments she
spends with her grandchildren.

Once upon a time, I knew a woman whose
grown children respect and call for
advice.

Once upon a time, I knew a woman whom I
met as a girl and knew as a woman, as a
mother, and now as a grandmother and
great grandmother.

# Endnotes

1. Duane A. Garrett, "Proverbs, Ecclesiastes, Song of Songs," Volume 14, *The New AmWillan Commentary* (Nashville, Tennessee: Broadman and Holman, 1993).

2. "Vince Lombardi - The Number One Speech," (CNBC, Sep 13, 2013, 4:33 p.m. EDT).

3. Mike Mason, *Mystery of Marriage: A Woman's Guide to Choosing a Great Husband* (Grand Rapids, MI: Zondervan, 1999).

4. Gordon MacDonald, *When Men Think Private Thoughts* (Nashville: Thomas Nelson, 1996).

5. Bill Bright, *The Four Spiritual Laws* (Orlando, FL: Cru, 1952).

6. Dictionary.com

7. 1 John 3:1, Ephesians 2:10, 1 Peter 2:9, Psalm 139:13–16, 1 Corinthians 3:16

8. Matthew 10:26–31

9. "Revealing Divorce Statistics in 2023," Christy Biever, J.D., *Forbes Advisor*, August 8, 2023.

10. Judith S. Wallerstein and Sandra Blakeslee, *Second Chances: Men, Women, and Children a Decade after Divorce* (New York: Ticknor & Fields, 1989).

11. Ken Boa, "Chapter 2: Relational Spirituality: Loving Ourselves Correctly," Conversatio Divina, September 23, 2020, https://conversatio.org/chapter-2-relational-spirituality-loving-ourselves-correctly/.

12. Letter from Dr. Kenneth Boa, Reflections Ministries (Atlanta, Georgia, December 2023).

# Acknowledgments

I would like to thank the following people:

Eldeen—my wife, partner, and supporter in the ministry the Lord has called me to. Your faithfulness to the Lord and to me over many decades has been a steadfast source of strength.

The many individuals who came into my counseling room with hope and expectations for change and encouragement during my forty-plus years of counseling—you have each left a mark on my life.

My friend Bill Little, whose encouragement moved me to put this book into print.

Kathleen Groom and the entire team at Book Journey who took my manuscript and brought it to life.

Dawn, Deanna, and Stuart Robb—my daughters and son. Each of you has contributed to my life in unique and meaningful ways.

My son-in-law, Blair, thank you for being present, contributing, and helping me in so many ways.

My daughter-in-law, Tiffany, who graciously helped with the tedious task of typing the manuscript into a Word document. Your effort made this possible.

Taylor, Chandler, McKenzie, Carter, and Samantha, along

with our grandchildren's husbands, Todd and Ben—watching you grow into young adults has been one of my greatest joys. I'm so blessed to see how each of you, in your own way, has grown in your relationship with the Lord Jesus.

Elle, our most precious great-granddaughter—I already see God's wisdom growing in your heart.

And finally, to you, the reader… may you discover the power and love of intimacy.

Above all, to the Lord Jesus Christ, who took what was weak in me and made me strong. All glory belongs to Him.

# Author Bio

G ENE SCHRADER, founder and director of North Atlanta Counseling Services (NACS), is a licensed Marriage and Family Therapist and a member of the American Association of Christian Counselors (AACC). He has been in private practice since 1977 with extensive experience in individual therapy, marriage and family therapy, teenage problems, and sexuality. Gene brings God's truth to those in conflict within their marriages, adjusting and grieving to losses in life, and depression.

As a speaker for church groups, Gene has conducted seminars on sexuality, bonding and true intimacy, parenting and fathering, overcoming affairs, and loyalty. Gene earned his master's degree in counseling from Georgia State University while also attending Psychological Studies Institute (a Christian psychological institute) in Atlanta.

Gene and his wife, Eldeen, have been married since 1963. They have three children, five grandchildren, and one great-granddaughter.

www.ingramcontent.com/pod-product-compliance
Lightning Source LLC
Chambersburg PA
CBHW051722260326
41914CB00031B/1692/J